# FREE Study Skills D~~VD~~ ~~~~

Dear Customer,

Thank you for your purchase from Mometrix! We consider it an honor and privilege that you have purchased our product and want to ensure your satisfaction.

As a way of showing our appreciation and to help us better serve you, we have developed a Study Skills DVD that we would like to give you for <u>FREE</u>. **This DVD covers our "best practices" for studying for your exam, from using our study materials to preparing for the day of the test.**

All that we ask is that you email us your feedback that would describe your experience so far with our product. Good, bad or indifferent, we want to know what you think!

To get your **FREE Study Skills DVD**, email <u>freedvd@mometrix.com</u> with "FREE STUDY SKILLS DVD" in the subject line and the following information in the body of the email:

    a.   The name of the product you purchased.

    b.   Your product rating on a scale of 1-5, with 5 being the highest rating.

    c.   Your feedback. It can be long, short, or anything in-between, just your impressions and experience so far with our product. Good feedback might include how our study material met your needs and will highlight features of the product that you found helpful.

    d.   Your full name and shipping address where you would like us to send your free DVD.

If you have any questions or concerns, please don't hesitate to contact me directly.

Thanks again!

Sincerely,

Jay Willis
Vice President
<u>jay.willis@mometrix.com</u>
1-800-673-8175

# Praxis II

## Business Education: Content Knowledge (5101) Exam

# SECRETS

## Study Guide
### Your Key to Exam Success

Praxis II Test Review for the
Praxis II: Subject Assessments

**Published by**
# Mometrix Test Preparation
Praxis II Exam Secrets Test Prep Team

Written and edited by the Praxis II Exam Secrets Test Prep Staff

Printed in the United States of America

This paper meets the requirements of ANSI/NISO Z39.48-1992 (Permanence of Paper).

Mometrix offers volume discount pricing to institutions. For more information or a price quote, please contact our sales department at sales@mometrix.com or 888-248-1219.

Praxis II® is a registered trademark of Educational Testing Services ® (ETS®), which was not involved in the production of, and does not endorse, this product.

ISBN 13: 978-1-62733-153-1
ISBN 10: 1-62733-153-0

Dear Future Exam Success Story:

Congratulations on your purchase of our study guide. Our goal in writing our study guide was to cover the content on the test, as well as provide insight into typical test taking mistakes and how to overcome them.

Standardized tests are a key component of being successful, which only increases the importance of doing well in the high-pressure high-stakes environment of test day. How well you do on this test will have a significant impact on your future, and we have the research and practical advice to help you execute on test day.

The product you're reading now is designed to exploit weaknesses in the test itself, and help you avoid the most common errors test takers frequently make.

## How to use this study guide

We don't want to waste your time. Our study guide is fast-paced and fluff-free. We suggest going through it a number of times, as repetition is an important part of learning new information and concepts.

First, read through the study guide completely to get a feel for the content and organization. Read the general success strategies first, and then proceed to the content sections. Each tip has been carefully selected for its effectiveness.

Second, read through the study guide again, and take notes in the margins and highlight those sections where you may have a particular weakness.

Finally, bring the manual with you on test day and study it before the exam begins.

## Your success is our success

We would be delighted to hear about your success. Send us an email and tell us your story. Thanks for your business and we wish you continued success.

Sincerely,

Mometrix Test Preparation Team

**Need more help? Check out our flashcards at: http://MometrixFlashcards.com/PraxisII**

# TABLE OF CONTENTS

# Top 20 Test Taking Tips

1. Carefully follow all the test registration procedures
2. Know the test directions, duration, topics, question types, how many questions
3. Setup a flexible study schedule at least 3-4 weeks before test day
4. Study during the time of day you are most alert, relaxed, and stress free
5. Maximize your learning style; visual learner use visual study aids, auditory learner use auditory study aids
6. Focus on your weakest knowledge base
7. Find a study partner to review with and help clarify questions
8. Practice, practice, practice
9. Get a good night's sleep; don't try to cram the night before the test
10. Eat a well balanced meal
11. Know the exact physical location of the testing site; drive the route to the site prior to test day
12. Bring a set of ear plugs; the testing center could be noisy
13. Wear comfortable, loose fitting, layered clothing to the testing center; prepare for it to be either cold or hot during the test
14. Bring at least 2 current forms of ID to the testing center
15. Arrive to the test early; be prepared to wait and be patient
16. Eliminate the obviously wrong answer choices, then guess the first remaining choice
17. Pace yourself; don't rush, but keep working and move on if you get stuck
18. Maintain a positive attitude even if the test is going poorly
19. Keep your first answer unless you are positive it is wrong
20. Check your work, don't make a careless mistake

# Accounting and Finance

### Assets

An asset is something that has or produces value and is owned. There are different types of assets. A fixed asset is a tangible asset that is generally used to generate profit and will not be turned into cash within the year. These may be known as "plant" and can include land, computer equipment, furniture, cars, buildings, and equipment used to build products. A variable asset may be transformed to cash sooner and will include the inventory of the actual product. It can also include accounts receivable, the money customers owe for delivered items. An intangible asset is not tangible—it's not physical. It includes recognition of the brand name as well as intellectual property like logos, trademarks, and patents. Though they aren't physical, intangible assets can be of high value.

### Liquidity, equity, depreciation, and cash flow

Liquidity refers to how easily an asset can be bought or sold on the market at the same price. It also refers to being able to make an asset become cash easily and quickly. Equity in a business shows what the owner has contributed in addition to the retained earnings. Basically it's the ownership minus the debts. Depreciation refers to how things lose value as time goes on. Cash flow refers to the actual cash that is going in and out of a business such as revenues or expenses due to business activities.

### GAAP

Generally accepted accounting principles (GAAP) provide a set of standards for how accounting figures and statements such as income statements, balance sheets, and cash flow statements are prepared. It is a set of rules that directs how these forms are prepared so that investors understand what they are getting when they receive the statements. It covers economic activity measurement, timing disclosures, and details on how financial statements are prepared and presented. It directs what financial information should be reported and makes it easier for investors to understand and compare companies. GAAP is required of many regulated companies by the US Securities and Exchange Commission (SEC) (many small businesses are excluded). The Financial Accounting Standards Board (FASB) issues GAAP through pronouncements.

### Cash and accrual accounting

The two major types of accounting systems are cash and accrual accounting. In cash accounting, the transactions are counted when the money is actually received or the expenses are paid out, regardless of when an item was ordered or delivered. Alternatively, in the accrual method, the transactions are counted when the orders are made or delivered, even if no cash has actually exchanged hands. For instance, if a furniture company sold and delivered a bed in January, but it was paid for in February, then the accrual method would record it in January and the cash method would show it in February. This affects where it is recorded for tax purposes. Most small businesses and individuals use the cash method but the larger ones may use the accrual method. The cash method is advantageous because it gives the company a better idea of cash on hand but may not show the correct profits, especially if a big sale has been made but not paid for. The accrual method shows the right profitability but may not give a good view of actual cash flow.

## Fundamental accounting equation

The fundamental accounting equation states that all assets = liabilities + owners' equity. It is used in double entry accounting and shown in the balance sheet, in which all assets can be added up as the equivalent of the liabilities and shareholder equality. When there is a purchase or sale, both sides will be affected equally. When a company buys an asset such as $100 in office supplies, then it will delete $100 of assets such as $100 of cash or it will be funded with shareholder equity or liabilities. This might be done by borrowing the money. When everything equals as it should, it is considered "balanced."

## Accounting cycle

The accounting cycle describes the steps taken in the accounting process. It is often shown as a circular diagram, thus the term "cycle." The first step is to attain all the source documents that are associated with financial transactions, including receipts, checks, and bank statements. Next, these transactions are analyzed to see how the accounts will be affected. The third step is to place entries into the journals for these transactions in a double-entry system. Next, the transactions are posted by moving them from the journals to the ledgers. An unadjusted trial balance is prepared showing the company's accounts. Next, the company will make adjusting entries as necessary. Account balances will go to where they should be. They will next prepare a trial balance with the adjustments in them. The company can then prepare financial statements such as the income statement. Closing entries are made as the balances of accounts that are temporary go to owner's equity. Finally, there is an after-closing trial balance.

### Ledgers and journals
Both ledgers and journals are quite important to the accounting cycle. Although they contain much of the same information, they are used differently. When a transaction occurs, it is first put into a journal. Transactions are put in based on when they occur. Journals can be for something specific, such as sales or purchases, or transactions may go into the general journal for less routine transactions like a bad debt or depreciation. The company will have a record of the transactions to which to refer. Later, the information is transferred to the ledger. The frequency of this varies. The ledger contains different accounts like asset accounts, revenue accounts, expense accounts, liability accounts, and equity accounts. The two types of ledgers include the general ledger and subsidiary (sub) ledgers. The ledgers are very important because documents such as income statements and balance sheets are produced from them. The exact use of journals and ledgers may be different in a computerized system.

## Double-entry bookkeeping, credits, and debits

With double-entry bookkeeping, two columns are used. All of the debits are placed on the left while the credits go on the right. Debts are recorded in the debit column as debits; these make assets and expense accounts go up and income, liability, and equity accounts go down. Likewise, credits make liability, income, and equity accounts go up and asset and expense accounts go down. The debits and credits always need to equal each other. When one changes, there should be another change to account for that. For instance, if a $10,000 car is bought with cash, then there should be a $10,000 car shown as an asset and a decrease in cash by $10,000. Therefore everything stays equal. It uses the fundamental accounting equation (assets = liabilities + owners' equity) as a basis.

## Trial balances

A trial balance is a document showing the ending balances of ledger accounts. It is done on a certain date as the company is preparing to create financial documents. On the top is the title, entity, and accounting period. Then the account titles are listed. Then there is a list of the debits (assets and expenses) on the left and a list of the credits (liabilities, income, and equity) on the right. The sum of the credits and debits are at the bottom. If everything is correct, these numbers should match, although they can still be inaccurate even if they do match. This can happen if incorrect entries were put into both the debit and credit sections at the same time, or if something was omitted altogether. Still, if they do not match, there is definitely a problem, and the company has a chance to investigate and fix it before creating the financial documents. If the company prepared the financial documents and then noticed the error, then the accountants would have to redo the documents, a much more arduous and time-consuming process. Accountants use the trial balance when making the financial documents.

## Manual and computerized accounting methods

Businesses can choose between manual and computerized accounting methods, and each has its advantages and disadvantages. In a manual system, people do the calculations on paper by hand; in a computerized system, they input them into a computer system. The actual formulas, calculations, and numbers are the same. Computerized systems are far quicker. The user simply enters the numbers and can have calculations and reports generated in an instant. It is very convenient. They can change numbers to see potential outcomes. This can minimize accidents one may make when calculating by hand. The business has to pay for the computer system, of course, but the money saved in labor hours might more than make up for this. Data can be easily backed up. Disadvantages are that there could be a computer malfunction that causes a loss of data. There could also be a security breach in which the information is leaked to the wrong person or hackers get in. If the data is entered incorrectly, even by a single digit, everything can be inaccurate. Most large businesses use a computerized system.

## Income statements

One of the most important financial documents is the income statement, which shows company profitability for a period of time. It contains many elements including revenues, gains, expenses, and losses. It lists revenues from primary activities (also known as operating revenues) such as sales revenues, service revenues, and revenues from secondary activities such as if a business earns interest or money from a source other than selling. It also lists gains such as long-term asset sales or lawsuits from something other than the primary activity. The income statement also shows expenses in primary activities, such as those used during normal operation, and expenses from secondary activities like interest. Losses from other sources should also be listed. This can occur if the company loses money on the sale of a long-term asset or suffers a lawsuit outside of normal transactions. The income statement will display the net profit or loss for the period of time it covers.

## Balance sheets

A balance sheet is one of the major financial documents, showcasing a moment in time. Essentially, it is a snapshot showing the financial situation of the company. It showcases assets, liabilities, and ownership equity, with the assumption that assets = liabilities + equity. It lists assets, which are things that have value, in the order of their liquidity. These may include things such as cash, accounts receivable, inventory, plant and equipment, investment property, and more. After that, it lists liabilities such as accounts payable, promissory notes, corporate bonds, deferred tax liabilities, and more. Next it shows equity, which is the net worth of the company's capital. It is the difference between assets and liabilities. The two forms of balance sheets are the report form and the account form. The balance sheet is very important for every business.

## Statements of retained earnings

The statement of retained earnings is a very important financial document, required when income statements and comparative balance sheets are given. It showcases how a business' retained earnings change over a period of time. Retained earnings are defined as a business' accumulated net income with the dividends that were given to stockholders subtracted. The information it contains is sourced from the income statement; subsequently, the information from the statement of retained earnings is used for the balance sheet. At the beginning is the starting balance. Factors like profits and dividend payments are added and subtracted to get the final retained earning balance. The general equation is starting retained earnings + net income – stockholder dividends = final retained earnings. Sometimes the statement gets into more detail by showing various types of retained earnings.

## Statements of cash flow

A cash flow statement is a major accounting document that outlines the influx and outflow of cash from a company. It is important because it shows what a company's cash position is, which can be different from its income if there are accounts that have not paid. It can show if the company is managing cash wisely or having difficulty with it. A cash flow statement covers cash gained and used in operating activities, investing activities, financing activities, and supplemental information. Operating activities convert the business' net income to cash basis with the balance changes in the current liability and current assets accounts. Investing activities include balance changes of long term assets like buildings and equipment. Financing activities includes balance changes in stockholders' equity and long-term liability accounts like preferred stock. Supplemental information shows interest, income taxes, and major non-cash exchanges. It will list each of these and show the increase or decrease in cash from each. At the end, it will show the net increase in cash from all, the cash at the beginning of the month, and finally the cash at the end of the month.

## Financial ratios

Liquidity ratios measure if a company can meet its obligations in the short term. The more liquid assets it has compared to short-term liabilities, the more liquid it will be. The current ratio is equal to the current assets divided by the current liabilities. The quick ratio formula is quick ratio = (cash + accounts receivable + marketable or short-term securities) / (current liabilities). This is a tougher test for liquidity. The cash ratio formula is cash = (cash + marketable or short-term securities) / (current liabilities). The higher these ratios are, the more liquid the firm is and the more likely it can reach its short-term debts. The debt to equity ratio shows the company's financial leverage. It is equal to total liabilities/shareholders equity. If it is high, a lot of debt has been used to finance growth. The return on equity (ROE) ratio is a percentage with the equation ROE = net income / shareholder's equity. It shows profitability. Activity ratios show how balance sheet accounts can be transformed into sales or cash. It shows a firm's efficiency. Two popular ones are the inventory turnover ratio and total assets turnover ratio.

## Payroll records

Payroll records must include a variety of components. It will contain identifying information such as the employee's name, social security number, address, birth date (for employees under 19), gender, and occupation. It may also contain the hiring letter, a pay authorization, the employee's W-4 form, payroll deduction forms, direct deposit forms, time sheets, records of attendance, W-2 forms, and all other forms related to payment. It will have the details of the compensation such as the wage base, pay rate per hour (if applicable), hours worked, dates, and more. It will also show deductions from the wages, such as taxes like income taxes, as well as contributions to retirement accounts or deductions for social security, healthcare expenses, and more. Many items are taken out of the pay before the employee receives them so the employee does not have to do so regularly.

## Payroll accounting procedures

Companies follow specific payroll accounting procedures to ensure accurate compensation and reporting. First, a company must have a way to compute the amount of time an employee works. Sometimes this is set to a schedule, whereas other times an hourly employee works different hours every day. A time card or electronic time clock may be used to keep track of this. Sometimes, employees keep their own records or are salaried and receive the same amount no matter how many hours they work. The pay must then be computed for each person. This may be a set amount based on a salary, or be the number of hours worked multiplied by the hourly rate. It may be more complicated and include other things such as investment account distributions, bonuses, or reimbursements. They must have a system to account for special time such as when the employee is taking paid leave. The company must compute and submit all applicable taxes such as income taxes on behalf of the employee and payroll taxes. They must make other deductions such as healthcare premiums. Once this is worked out, the company will distribute the money. This is often done by check or direct deposit.

## Periodic and perpetual inventory systems

Two major types of inventory systems are periodic and perpetual inventory systems. In perpetual inventory systems, the inventory changes and cost of goods sold are updated in real time as the item is sold. Other inventory changes, such as returns, are also recorded immediately. In a periodic system, a purchases account record is changed when the purchase is made, but the cost of goods sold and inventory doesn't change until the accounting period closes. Perpetual inventory systems are very popular, especially with the increase in technology point-of-sale systems. They allow businesses to always know what inventory they have and restock as necessary. They provide much more useful and updated information. The disadvantage is that it can cost a lot of money to initially put in the technology for a perpetual inventory system. Some small businesses do not have the money or ability to do this.

## Inventory costing systems

### FIFO and LIFO methods

Inventory costing is the process of assigning a cost to a particular item. There are various methods a company can use. With the first in, first out (FIFO) method, the oldest cost is assigned to the first item sold, then the next oldest cost to the next item sold, and so on. For instance, if five shirts were bought wholesale for $10, and then next five were bought for $12, then the first five sold would have the $10 cost and the next five would have the $12 cost, even if they weren't the ones actually bought for those amounts. This is very common because it is a good approximation of the real

- 6 -

world. With the last in, first out (LIFO) method, it is the opposite and the most recent cost is assigned to the first items sold. In this case it would be $12 for the first five shirts sold and then $10. This is used less often.

<u>Average cost and specific identification methods</u>
The average cost and specific identification methods are two inventory costing methods. The average cost method keeps a running average of inventory and assigns the item sold the current average. For instance, if a company buys five shirts for $10 and five for $12, then the next shirt sold would be assigned the cost of $11. This is good when a company has non-perishable items that are not sold sequentially. It can be steadier and more reliable as long as there is not a great change in the costs of the items. The specific identification method assigns the cost of a product with the actual cost paid for that specific product. These are used for low-volume, high-dollar producers. For instance, a company that sells high-end cars might use this system so they know exactly how much they made on a car. It is not good for companies with a lot of very similar items.

## Depreciation

Depreciation is the concept that assets such as equipment, machinery, and cars have a useful life and will only be usable for a certain amount of time and therefore depreciate (or lose value) as time goes on. This is used in accounting. There might be a residual value to the asset, or a value at the end. For instance, imagine a company buys a truck for $110,000 and expects it to have a 10-year useful life. At the end of the 10 years, they expect to be able to sell it for $10,000. They may use the straight line method of depreciation in which they simply average the depreciation across the years. For every year, they will show a depreciation expense of $10,000. Businesses can use this as an income tax deduction as long as it meets all the criteria.

## Management accounting

Management accounting refers to the evaluation of information for the purpose of managers. It can include the identification, measurement, evaluation, interpretation, and communication of information. Its main goal is to help managers make decisions about the business. This is different than financial accounting, which is done to give information to outside parties. In management accounting, management accounts are created that have financial information suitable for managers. Managers use these to make short-term decisions. Elements that may be included in these reports include sales reports numbers, cash available, order amount, sales revenue, inventory reports, accounts payable and receivable accounts, trend charts, and more. Managers can get an idea of how projects will progress, understand how business choices will affect the business financially, oversee finances, and more.

## Cost accounting

Cost accounting is useful for managers to help make decisions while planning and controlling. It looks at the costs of different items such as products and projects. To accomplish this, both the input costs of production and the fixed costs are considered. Once input and output are measured, these can be compared to see how the item is performing financially. This can help managers make a decision on whether to continue with the project or product and ways they can improve it. It analyzes many things such as cost-volume-profit connections, activity-based costing, and cost behavior. It helps managers decide how much to charge for certain processes or services because they will know how much it cost.

## Types of costs

Direct costs are the costs that go directly into making a product. For instance, if a company is manufacturing pens, then the cost of the ink would be a direct cost. An indirect cost is incurred to the company as a whole and is necessary but not directly tied into that one product. For instance, the office supplies used in the marketing department would be an indirect cost. They are not used directly in making the pens, but they are still important to the function of the marketing department that helps to promote the pen. Fixed costs are costs that stay the same. For instance, the cost of a salaried employee would be a fixed cost because it is always the same. No matter how many pens are made, it stays the same. Variable costs can change, however. For instance, if the pen making machine uses more electricity when it makes more pens, then this would be a variable cost. Companies work to minimize these costs while maximizing efficiency.

## Methods to evaluate financial performance

A cost-volume-profit analysis (CVP) is part of managerial economics and looks at how alterations in the cost (fixed and variable) and sales volume change the profit of a company. A break-even analysis calculates when the expenses of a company are covered and there is a profit. The general equation for this is breakeven point = fixed costs / (selling price of a unit - variable costs). The return on investment (ROI) shows an investment's efficiency. It is calculated with the following equation: ROI = (gain derived from investment – cost of the investment) / cost of the investment. The answer is a percentage. A company can use this to compare different projects. Managers might not want to continue a project that has a negative ROI. Likewise, when comparing two projects, they would look for the one with the higher ROI. It is a simple but powerful equation. Companies will often use multiple strategies to evaluate financial performance.

## Creating a personal budget

A personal budget can be created through a series of straightforward steps. First, one should set a manageable time span for the budget. Once the timing is set, the individual should formulate his ultimate financial goals. Creating a financial reserve is important in case there is an unexpected expense. He should decide how much money he wants to have left for his reserve or other savings. Next, the individual should calculate income. He must be careful to take out money for taxes, interest, and automatic fees. He should then make budget line items for recurring fees that are unavoidable such as rent, mortgage payments, car payments, etc. Next, he should add in needs such as food. He should consider how much he spends in each category and formulate ways to save. He should then add in other items such as leisure activities and unnecessary items. As time passes, he can make adjustments as necessary.

## Selecting a bank, savings plan, and checking account

Banks vary greatly in the accounts, programs, and financial tools they offer, thus consumers should spend time comparing them to find the best for them. First, individuals should consider their banking needs. They might want a checking account, which typically pays little to no interest, but allows people to easily withdraw by writing checks. Alternatively, they may want a savings account that doesn't allow for checks but which offers interest. The characteristics of these accounts differ greatly. Factors that should be evaluated include fees, minimums, interest rates on accounts, services, special features, and more. They should also evaluate customer service. Some banks might be better for one product and worse for another, so people should evaluate exactly what they need.

In addition, services, prices, fees, and other details change very often, so people should evaluate their options right before they are ready to commit to a banking product.

## Investment options

Securities
Securities are financial assets that can be traded. These investments include many different types, including stocks and bonds, and are not tangible items. Bonds and banknotes are two common types of debt securities. With debt securities, the investor is the lender. Equity securities are stocks in which the investor purchases a small portion of a company. Securities are advantageous because they can provide a great deal of return on an investor's money. Especially with securities like stocks, an investor can do very well. A disadvantage is that they often involve risk. With some of them, an investor can lose everything. Securities range in both risk and return; in general the greater the risk, the greater the potential for a large return. Investors may get a certificate or an electronic form.

Bonds
Investing in bonds means an investor is loaning money to an institution, which is borrowing the money. In exchange, the borrower is providing the investor (or lender) with a coupon or premium. Thus, the investor will get money for lending this money. In addition, when the bond reaches maturity, its face value will be given back to the investor. The advantage of bonds is that they are a less risky form of investing than many other methods such as stocks. Most of the time, investors receive the money they are promised. The disadvantage is that the return does not generally have the potential to be as great as with stocks. While stocks can return an almost unlimited amount, bonds are limited greatly. They offer less risk, but less reward. Many people invest in a combination of bonds and stocks.

Stocks
Stocks are a common form of investment. With stocks, investors purchase a very small amount of a company. The returns they generally see are from rising stock prices when the company is doing well. Sometimes the company pays dividends as well. Stocks can be advantageous in that there is no limit to what someone can make. If they choose a stock in a company that skyrockets, they can literally make a fortune on a small investment. The downside is that there can be a lot of risk. Just as the stock price can rise dramatically, it can also go down dramatically and become practically worthless. Thus, an investor could lose everything. Some stocks are riskier than others, and diversifying lowers the risk.

Mutual funds
Mutual funds are businesses that take money from a variety of investors and put it in a portfolio of bonds, stocks, securities, and assets. Each mutual fund has a different combination. A person who buys into a mutual fund will hold a portion of ownership of the portfolio and reap the rewards when the portfolio gains value. The idea is that an investor enjoys diversification by not investing in one single asset. There is risk involved with mutual funds—they can lose value—and there are fees and other costs that can lower the value. The government does not guarantee them. Some are riskier than others, depending on the combination of the portfolio. Still, they are a good way to balance risk and reward and are a popular retirement and investment option.

## Taxes individuals may face

Personal income taxes are taxes on the money a person earns. The federal government applies these, as do some states. Individuals pay a percentage of their income (after deductions and credits). The percentage is based on how much they make and goes up as income rises. The Federal Insurance Contributions Act (FICA) and Medicare taxes fund the federal programs of social security and Medicare, which provide money and health benefits to senior citizens, the disabled, and other eligible individuals. Property taxes are levied on properties and are generally based on the amount the property is worth. Gains taxes are based on profit from a non-inventory asset such as bonds, stocks, property, and precious metals. Sales taxes are paid on items people buy. Individuals must prepare income tax returns yearly, and many use an accountant to do so. They can look for deductions such as dependents, charitable contributions, or business expenses, which can reduce the amount of wages eligible to be taxed. They can also claim credits, which reduce the taxes owed. Contributing to retirement plans can also reduce taxes. Some owe, while others enjoy a refund.

## Types of credit individuals may possess

Credit cards allow people to make purchases in advance and then pay it back monthly. People can keep a balance on the cards, but the interest can be very high. Auto loans are loans that are tied to cars. They allow people to pay off their cars slowly, but they could lose the car if they can't pay. Mortgages are loans made to let people purchase homes. Generally these come from the bank and allow homebuyers to slowly pay off the house with interest. Foreclosure could occur if the loan is not repaid. Student loans help students pay for education. Home equity loans are loans in which the person's home equity is put up as collateral in case the person defaults on the loan. People may use this for large expenses. A variable loan is a loan in which the interest rate changes along with the market interest rate, changing the payments. Alternatively, a fixed interest rate loan has the interest rate stay the same during the life of the loan. How high the interest rates are and the length of the loan determine which is best.

## Factors that could affect personal credit

Bankruptcy has a major impact on personal credit. Chapter 7, 11 and 13 bankruptcies remain on credit reports for as long as a decade, although Chapter 13 may come off in seven years. Negative reports about delinquent accounts that lower credit may stay for seven years, although positive closed accounts can stay for longer. Credit can go down with collections and these can stay for seven years, as well. Credit score can even be slightly lowered when an individual just applies for credit and this can last two years. Late payments also lower credit rating. Balances on credit cards can cause credit rating to drop, thus if an individual is only making minimum payments, he will have a lower credit rating and thus less ability to get and use credit. Inflation may make it harder for some people to pay their credit cards. Credit cards are governed by many laws and regulations.

## Methods for managing personal credit and debt

Consumers should work to manage personal credit and debt. They should try to get rid of unhealthy, high-cost debt such as credit card debt by paying off loans and balances. They can start by creating a budget. They should separate things into needs and wants and try to focus on only the needs until they have managed their debt. They should not buy things they cannot afford. People can also try to increase their income. People may also be able to talk to the creditors and come up with a payment plan or a reduction in the debt, which will make it easier to pay back. They should try to do this as soon as possible before a debt collector begins to make collection calls. There are debt relief services that offer credit counseling. These can be very useful, but consumers should be careful because many involve scams. Debt management plans and debt settlement programs can be done if researched properly (again, there are a lot of scams out there) and if there aren't other options. This may help get a person out of unmanageable debt.

## True costs of credit

Credit has a much higher cost than many consumers realize, especially if they are only paying the minimum amount and have high interest on credit cards. The cost of the interest is based on the annual percentage rate (APR) and the amount. For instance, if someone buys a television for $100 on a credit card with 20 percent APR and paid it in one year, then they would pay $120. The interest would be the APR multiplied by the principal amount. This calculates to $100 × 20% (0.2), or $20 interest. Sometimes the credit cards have such a low monthly minimum payment that it does not even cover the interest. If people are only paying the minimum, they might continue to owe more and more money. For instance, if in the last example the minimum payment was only $10 a year, then after the year, the consumer would still owe $110. Then the interest for that year would be $110 × 20%, or $22. The exact cost of the credit depends on APR and how long it takes a person to repay the loan.

## Life insurance

Life insurance is a type of coverage people buy that pays out upon a person's death. Whole life insurance is also an investment. When the person passes away, a fixed amount is paid out. This builds cash value each year and can be borrowed against. Term life insurance does not have an investment component. People will buy it for a certain amount of time and pay a monthly premium. This can be very inexpensive for someone who is young. There are many life insurance terms. A beneficiary is the person who receives the money upon the insured person's death. A rider changes provisions or clauses of the insurance policy. Annuities give a regular income. Most of the time these are for life. Actuarial tables show the chances that someone will pass away before their birthday, used by life insurance companies when developing plans and pricing. Those shopping for life insurance should familiarize themselves with all the concepts prior to choosing.

## Factors that affect the decision whether to carry life insurance

First, an individual should consider who is counting on his income. A single person who lives alone and does not support anyone else might not need life insurance, whereas a father who is the sole support for three young children would need it much more. When the person is the breadwinner in the family or has dependents that count on him, he (or she) is much more likely to need the life insurance. If someone else would be able to get a job and provide the income, the need would be reduced. The person should consider how long others will depend on the income. Someone with very young children would need it more than someone with older children who are self-sufficient. The needs of the people depending on the income also matter. For instance, if one of the children has a disability and will incur expensive long-term medical bills, life insurance is more important. A person should also consider long term savings. Someone who has a lot of savings that can be used to support dependents will need less life insurance than someone who relies on every paycheck.

## Auto and property insurance

Automobile insurance covers drivers in the case of an occurrence that causes some sort of damage or harm. Many states force drivers to have insurance. There are many different types of policies with different coverage levels. Liability coverage provides benefits to damages suffered by other drivers. Collision coverage is for cars involved in an accident. People often have a deductible, or money they have to pay first. Premiums are the amount a driver pays monthly or regularly to maintain coverage. Comprehensive insurance also covers cars damaged without a collision such as from vandalism or weather-related events. Property insurance provides coverage against a wide variety of risks and includes fire insurance, earthquake insurance, home insurance, and flood insurance. Open perils is a type that includes all causes except those exempted, whereas named perils lists the types of causes for the insurance. There are many plans with different premiums, coverage, deductibles, and exclusions. Replacement insurance will give benefits so people can replace the lost items, whereas actual cash value takes off for depreciation. People should evaluate the potential risk and costs of insurance when deciding on the plan that is right for them.

## Health insurance

Health insurance is very important for individuals and families to help pay for medical expenses. People typically pay a monthly fee or premium for coverage. They may have to pay a deductible, or an amount of money before the insurance company pays. Sometimes there are out-of-pocket limits or the maximum amount the consumer has to pay. There are many sources of health insurance. Many people get an employer-sponsored plan from their place of work. Others may get a private plan in the marketplace. Some may receive it from the government through Medicare or Medicaid. Still others might find it from a different source. There are many different types of plans. A PPO is a preferred provider plan, which generally gives greater benefits if an individual sees someone "in network" as compared to "out of network." An HMO contracts physicians, hospitals, and other providers and gives benefits based on that. When choosing health insurance, people should consider current and potential healthcare concerns, the dependents who also need coverage, the premium, the coverage the plans offer, deductibles, limits, exclusions, and more. Plans vary in all these aspects.

## Strategies to make the best purchase decisions

First, it is important for people to research the products they are considering. The Internet makes it easy to read ratings and reviews to compare the features, benefits, and prices of different products. There is often a quality versus price trade-off, but not always. If there is one, it is not always significant, especially if someone is paying more for a brand name. People can also do research by looking at product labels so they know exactly what they are getting. People should comparison shop. Oftentimes the same item can be found for far less from a particular source. They can look at advertisements to find the best deals, but they need to be wary. Advertisements are not always as good a deal as they claim, thus consumers should be sure to read the fine print. Consumers should also investigate any service plans and warranties offered to ascertain their value. The more research a consumer does, the better the chance of getting the right product at the right price.

## Factors that affect total cost of purchase

Many factors affect a purchase's total cost beyond the retail price. A consumer must consider taxes on the product as well as fees. Some products, such as cars, often have other fees. A person must consider what else they may need to purchase to be able to use the product. For instance, a person cannot operate a car without a license tag. The cost of credit, if applicable, needs to be considered. If someone is financing a car, then they will pay more than the retail price because they will pay interest on the money. The costs to operate should be considered. A car needs gas, so this is an additional cost that will be incurred. A car also needs maintenance. A person should consider how long the life of the product will be. Most cars do not last 20 years. The person should consider how many years of life the product will deliver when getting an idea of the cost. By considering all of these different factors, a consumer can get a better idea of the true cost of a product.

## Strategies for lowering product's cost

Consumers can save a great deal of money with various strategies for lowering a product's cost. First, they can take advantage of sales. Sales allow consumers to save a great amount of money on products, and many stores have significant sales such as buy one, get one free. Certain days such as holidays are often accompanied by sales. Consumers can also look for coupons for both traditional store and online purchases. They can purchase items on clearance for even greater savings. Another option is to purchase in bulk. Consumers will generally get a lower per item cost by doing this. Consumers can also comparison shop to look for the lowest price on an item. This is easy to do on the Internet. They can shop at discount stores and/or low priced websites to save money. These strategies can be combined for even greater savings.

## Ascertaining needs and resources before large purchases

Consumers should ascertain both their needs and resources before making large purchases. They may find that they do not need to make such a large purchase, but can instead make do with a less expensive option. They may also discover they have other items that can substitute for the purchase they were about to make. Consumers also need to consider their resources. Products may cost more than the retail price when one considers tax, other fees and interest on a credit card. They need to make sure they can afford it. By taking these measures, consumers will not spend more than is wise and will make the most of their money.

## Factors that can influence employment opportunities

Economic factors can have a significant impact on employment opportunities. When the economy is doing well, businesses will also be doing well and may be more likely to be expanding and hiring new people. When the economy is doing poorly, a person may have more difficulty finding a job. There may be a lot more supply (people looking for jobs) than demand (jobs hiring). This ranges by job—certain jobs, such as nurses, will always have openings. Geographic location also makes a large difference in employment opportunities. There are many more opportunities for businessmen in New York City than in a small town in rural America. The opportunities also vary by industry. Certain locations have more opportunities for certain positions. There are many personal factors that influence an individual's employment opportunities such as education, skills, and experience.

## Factors that influence cost of living

One factor that influences the cost of living is the housing prices. Housing prices can vary a great deal and can change by many percentage points, even while salaries remain relatively stagnant. When housing prices go up, so does the cost of living. This can vary greatly depending on the area. A person's family size greatly affects his cost of living. Kids are expensive, with costs such as medical bills, housing costs, food, education, and so forth. Someone with a larger family will have a greater cost of living. Inflation also influences the cost of living. When there is high inflation, the cost of living can go up. Things will cost more and a person may not make more money. This can make it more difficult to afford the basics.

## Factors that influence personal income

A person's education influences their personal income. Someone with a higher degree, such as a master's degree or doctorate, will generally make more than someone with a lower degree or someone without a degree at all. Many of the companies with higher paying jobs want people with higher education. In some fields they look for people with certifications. Experience also matters—those with more experience will generally earn more money. Someone who is skilled will earn more money, especially if the skills are particularly unique or valuable. Factors outside the person, such as the job market, also affect income. The prevailing wages in that field make a large difference. Also, when the economy is doing well and a lot of people are hiring, a person might earn more. The geographic location also makes a difference. An employee will generally earn more in a place like New York City as compared to a small town. A higher cost of living will balance some of that.

## Annual profits from sales data

Companies calculate annual profit to ascertain how much money they have brought in through the year. The first step in getting the annual profit is to add up all of the revenues. This may include sales from different products or other sources of income. Next, all of the costs for the year must be added together. This may include many different types of costs. Companies need to subtract to account for returns. They need to consider all expenses, including but not limited to operating expenses, depreciation expenses, interest, etc. Finally, they will take the total costs and subtract that from the total income. This will give the profit. For instance, if a company has revenues of $100,000 and costs of $50,000, then it made $50,000 in profit. One of the best ways to get all the data for this calculation is from the income statement, which lists revenues and expenses.

## Profit margins

The profit margin statistic makes it possible to compare companies of different sizes because it is expressed as a percentage. To calculate profit margin, first the raw profit is calculated. This is done by subtracting total costs from sales revenue. For instance, if sales of a product made $10,000 for the company and costs were $8,000, then raw profit will be $10,000 - $8,000, or $2,000. Next, the gross profit is divided by the revenue. Thus $2,000 would be divided by $10,000 for an answer of 0.2. The profit margin is this number expressed as a percentage. To get this, a person would multiply the decimal by 100, thus 0.2 is equal to a 20 percent profit margin.

## Sale prices

The sale price of an item is the price minus the discount, which is calculated by the percentage off. To calculate the discount, one should multiply the percentage off and the full price. For instance, to calculate the sale price of an item that is $100 and 20 percent off, first the percentage should be transformed to decimal form, which is done by moving the decimal point to the left by two digits. Thus 20 percent is the same as 0.2, five percent is the same as 0.05, and one percent is the same as 0.01. To calculate the discount, one would multiple 0.2 by 100. This equals $20. The sale price is calculated by taking the full price and subtracting the discount. In this example, it is $100 - $20. Thus the sale price is $80.

## Commissions

Many employees are paid on commission, thus it is important to understand how to properly calculate them. First, the employee must understand the amount of money that is eligible for commission. For instance, a salesman might receive commissions when selling certain products but not others. Some people get a commission on sales while others receive profit-based commissions. Next, employees should ascertain the percentage commission they receive. This may vary. For instance, a salesman might receive a different percentage of commission depending on what they sell. Once he knows the commissionable amount and rate of commission, he will then multiply them together. For instance, if an employee receives a 10 percent commission on $100, then he will receive $10 in commission (0.1 × $100). The employee will then need to calculate taxes on the commission to ascertain his final pay.

## Hourly wages from an annual full-time salary

It is simple to calculate hourly wages from an annual full-time salary. First, the amount of hours worked in the year must be calculated. If the person worked 40 hours a week, then the number of hours worked in the year would be 40 × 52, or 2080 hours. If they worked 35 hours a week, then it would be 35 × 52, or 1820. Generally, full-time indicates a 40-hour work week, so 2080 should be assumed if there is no other information except that it is full-time. To calculate the hourly wage, simply divide the full-time salary by 2080. Thus if the person earned $41,600, then the hourly salary would be $41,600 / 2080, or $20 an hour.

## Percentages

To calculate a percentage from a decimal, one has to simply multiply it by 100. Thus, 0.15 is 15 percent. To increase a number by a certain percentage (like when a product is marked up by a percentage), a person would first calculate the increase by multiplying the percentage by the cost. For instance, if the cost of a good is $100 and the company wants to mark it up 50 percent, then the markup would be $100 multiplied by 50 percent (which is the same as 0.5), and that would equal $50. Thus the cost plus the markup would be $150. A person can also use it to find wholesale prices. If the wholesale price is 75 percent of the price of $100, then to get the wholesale price, a person would just multiply $100 by 75% or 0.75 to get a wholesale price of $75. Percentages are used in many business applications.

## Frequency distributions

Frequency distributions are tables that show how often specific results emerged. For instance, a teacher might do a frequency table showing how often the students got an A, B, C, D or F. The teacher would create the table listing the grades on the left and then put the number of students that achieved each one to the right. To find out how many earned a grade, the person could look at the table. Frequency tables are used often in business. For instance, if one needed to find out how often sales reached a certain level, he (or she) could put the data into a frequency table and see how often that occurred. Some frequency tables will also list a cumulative total; this is good if the person wanted to see how often sales reached at least a certain level.

## Common statistics

Mean is simply the average of a group of numbers. This is calculated by adding all the numbers and dividing by how many numbers there are. For instance, if the numbers are 3, 2, 3, and 4, one would add them to get 12 and then divide by 4 to get 3 as the mean. The mode is simply the number that appears the most. In the group 3, 2, 3, and 4, the number 3 is the mode because it appears twice. The median is the number that would appear in the middle if the numbers were put in order. If the numbers are 7, 3, 9, 1, 5, the numbers would be put in order to 1, 3, 5, 7, 9, and the mode would be 5 because that is in the middle. To get the standard deviation, the mean should be calculated first. Take each number and subtract the mean, then get the squared difference by squaring the result. Finally, take all the squared differences in the group and find their average. That is the standard deviation.

## Line graphs

A line graph shows the connection between information. It is often used to show changes over time. For instance, a company may want to show how sales changed from month to month. On the vertical axis, they would label the different sales levels, including both the lowest and highest possible amount. On the horizontal axis, the months would be listed. For every month, a dot would be placed on the sales level. Once all the dots are posted for the different months, a line would be drawn to connect the dots to more easily show the relationship. In this case, mangers could see whether sales went up, went down, stayed stagnant, or had no general pattern as the months went by. Line graphs can be useful visual aids for businesses.

## Scatter plots

A scatter plot shows how two variables are related to each other. A company can plot the different values of the variables to see how they relate. For instance, a company may want to see how sales are at different price points. On the vertical axis they can put sales while on the horizontal one they can put price. They can then adjust the price of their product and figure out the sales level for one day of each price. They will then plot the numbers on the graph and look for a relationship. Depending on the variables, there may or may not be one. In this case, the expected relationship will be that the higher the price, the lower the sales. They can use the graph to work out what is the best price point to make the best profits. Scatter plots can give a good visual representation of the relationship between two variables and are often used in business.

## Bar graphs

A bar graph can be used to show data in a way that is clear and easy to understand. The first step is the title. For instance, a baseball coach may create a bar graph of hits made by players, and this can be the title. Next, a label for each axis must be given. There will be a grouped data axis representing the groups such as "Baseball Players." This can be either the horizontal or vertical axis. In this case, it will be at the bottom of the graph. A label should be created for the frequency axis such as "Number of Hits." This should be on the left side of the graph. A range also needs to be produced. If the best hitter had 18 hits, then the scale might go from 0-20. The scale interval should be considered. There could be one mark for each hit or a marker to signify every five hits. Now the data is used to draw in bars to the correct height. For instance, the player that made 10 hits will have a bar that rises to the 10 marker. This will be repeated for all the players.

## Circle graphs

Circle graphs are useful visual aids that show a variety of data. First, a circle is formed. Then the circle is divided into different sectors to represent the different elements that the graph is representing. The sectors should be the size of their percentage. For instance, a company might make a circle graph representing sales of different colors of a product like a shirt. If half of consumers bought the blue shirt, then half the circle would be a segment representing the blue shirt. If a quarter bought the red shirt, then a quarter of the circle would be a sector representing the red. Once all the sectors are created, they should be labeled with what they represent and the corresponding percentage. The business can then view the graph to easily get an idea of which colors sold the best.

## Addition, subtraction, multiplication, and division

With addition, students simply add the amount of each to calculate the total number. For instance, if one person has five apples and another has five more, the total is 10. With subtraction, students start at a number and take away a certain amount. For instance, if one person has 10 apples and he gives away five, then he has five left. With multiplication, the person adds one of the numbers to itself the number of times of the second number. For instance, to multiply four times five, one would add four to itself five times. Thus $4 + 4 + 4 + 4 + 4 = 20$. To divide, a person calculates how many of one number fits in another number. Thus to solve $20 / 4$, a person would see that there are five 4s that would fit in 20, thus the answer is 5.

## Area, volume, and weight

To calculate the area of a rectangle, the formula $A = w \times l$ should be used in which A = area, w = width and l = length. For a triangle, the area is $\frac{1}{2} \times b \times h$, where b = base and h = height. For a circle the area is $\pi \times r^2$ where r = radius. The volume of a rectangular prism is $V = l \times w \times h$, where l = length, w = width and h = height. To calculate the volume of a cylinder, multiply $\pi \times r^2 \times h$. The formula for weight is $W = m \times g$, where m = mass and g = acceleration of gravity, which on Earth is $9.8 \text{ m/s}^2$.

## Compound interest

Compound interest is when interest gets added back to the principal and then interest is calculated on that additional amount when the next compounding period happens. The formula to calculate compound interest is $A = P (1 + r / n) \wedge nt$. In this formula, A represents the investment's future value (with interest). P is the principal or initial investment. R is the annual interest rate expressed as a decimal. N represents how many times the interested is compounded annually. T is how long the money has been invested (in years). For instance, if an amount of $10,000 was invested, the interest rate was 0.1 and it is compounded monthly, then after 20 years, the investment value would be $A = 10000 (1 + 0.1 / 12) \wedge 12 (20)$, which equals $73,280.74.

## Sampling techniques and selection

There are different methods of sampling used when doing research. The basic categories are probability sampling, in which every individual has a chance of getting selected in a known probability; and nonprobability sampling, in which some units may not have a chance of selection, or their probability isn't known. Simple random sampling is the best probability method, but is often very difficult to achieve. Every individual in the population has the same chance of being selected. Systemic sampling (also known as Nth name selection technique) takes every Nth individual from the population. With stratified sampling, the population is divided into stratums, or groups with a shared characteristic such as gender or age. These are matched against how many actually reside in the population. Then the researcher uses random sampling to take the number from each stratum that represents its presence in the population. With convenience sampling, the researcher finds a convenient sample. This is not as accurate as other methods. With judgment sampling, the researcher uses his judgment to find the sample. Quote sampling starts out like stratified sampling but, instead of random sampling, they use judgment or convenience sampling to pick the individuals from the stratums.

# Communication and Career Development

## Goals of business correspondence

There are a number of goals commonly seen on business correspondence, and at times they overlap. One of the major goals of business correspondence is to give information. One employee may be providing information to another employee, or the company may be sharing business happenings to customers. Another common goal is to sell the company's goods and services. Many companies create advertisements, blogs, social media posts, and other promotional materials to convince consumers to purchase their offerings. Business correspondence may also be used to convince an audience of something. A person may send a letter to a client to convince him that his product is better. An employee may try to convince another employee to try a new policy. Businessmen often correspond as a response to a question. If a consumer emails a question, customer service will respond with the answer. Businesses will often send out confirmation emails. This may be in response to a purchase or a question. Another form of correspondence may be sent out if an adjustment needs to be made. Correspondence may be through paper, email, the Internet, or other methods.

## Communication modalities

There are many different communication modalities used within a business, including emails, phone calls, and in-person meetings, each with its own uses. Face-to-face communication is very important in business, especially when delivering important or serious information. For instance, if there is a serious conflict with an employee, the supervisor is going to want to sit down and talk to him (or her). If a business is going after a big client, a face-to-face meeting can show a lot of effort. Meetings can impart a lot of information to many people very quickly, engage people, and allow everyone to interact. Email is used very often for a wide variety of business matters because of its ease, speed, and convenience. This is often used in customer service because many customers prefer it. Also, it allows customers and customer service to interact even when the customer is not available during service business hours. The telephone is also commonly used, especially when it is a quick question that needs immediate attention. If there is a lot of back and forth required, a phone call can be quicker than an exchange of emails. Companies generally use many of these forms of communication.

## Effective communication skills

Effective communication skills are important in business. First, it is important for people to practice active listening. This means perceiving everything about the communication by using all senses. Not only should a person listen with their ears, but they should watch for body language and try to evaluate how the speaker feels. People want to feel like others are really listening to them and processing what they are saying. Eye contact is important. The person shouldn't interrupt or make it seem like he's making judgments. He (or she) should display interest. This can be done by nodding or making small comments. Nonverbal communication is also important. The person should appear engaged, relaxed, and open. He should not be fidgeting. He should use open body language. A person should be aware of what he says and how it comes across, choosing his words carefully. One can easily insult someone, even accidently. He should not argue, but try to work together to communicate effectively. In business, people should think logically and try to keep stress and emotion from influencing decisions. With practice, people can improve their communication skills.

## Nonverbal communication

Nonverbal communication can be just as important as verbal communication in business, thus it is important to know the best strategies to make it effective. First, eye contact is important because it shows that a person is interested and engaged. It shows that he (or she) is listening. A person's facial expression can express a lot. When one smiles, he is showing friendliness, encouragement and/or satisfaction with the work. When one frowns or displays an angry face, it shows displeasure. It is important to show the expression that matches the feelings a person wants to convey when communicating in business, because otherwise the recipient may get the wrong idea. Gestures can show a lot. Someone clenching his fists may show anger. Hand movements can also help convey information. A person's posture tells a lot. Someone who crosses their arms may show resistance. Alternatively, someone may appear relaxed. A businessman who is standing or sitting tall may show off confidence. If someone is fidgeting, he may show discomfort or nervousness, which is not good for business. Businessmen should evaluate their nonverbal communication to make sure it enhances what they want to portray.

## Proper etiquette in personal and business communication

Individuals should always practice proper courtesy. Businessmen should ordinarily address each other in a formal way and conduct appropriate cultural moves such as shaking hands. It is important to practice cultural sensitivity and know the rules and traditions of the person being greeted. For instance, in some cultures one may bow, while in another they may hug. People should make every effort not to show any bias or stereotypes as this can be very insulting to business contacts. Sometimes someone will think they are being insulted when the person is simply ignorant of cultural customs. It is important to study the culture before interaction to make sure this does not happen. Otherwise, business communication should be formal and free of insults. It should be professional and without errors, as well.

## Communication types commonly seen in business

Business letters are sent for a wide variety of reasons and can be very formal. These may contain confidential and important information. Memoranda are a less formal method of communication and may be used for announcements, information dissemination, and directions. They may be sent to a lot of people at once and are generally short and to the point. Emails are now commonly used in business communications because of their ease of use and speed. These may be less formal than written out business letters, or they can be just as formal. Publicity materials are used to publicize an event or garner support. This may be something such as a press release. Recruitment communications are used in the process of hiring employees. For instance, a classified ad may be made when the company is hiring. Companies also make a lot of advertisements to draw consumers. These may be flashy advertisements or more subdued forms of communication and may appear in places such as newspapers and magazines.

## Terminology commonly used in business communication

A memorandum is a short, informal form of business communication used to disseminate information. When a company writes "Enclosures," it means there is/are one or more enclosures. In email, an attached file is an attachment. The return address is the address of the person sending the letter. The inside address, or letter mailing address, is the recipient's address. The salutation is the greeting used, very commonly "Dear." The body is the main content of the letter. The complementary close is the closing at the bottom of the letter. There may also be reference initials at the end of the letter, which refer to the person who actually typed it, if different than the writer. Knowing these terms can help an individual write a professional business letter.

## Writing business letters

A business letter should follow conventional professional practices. It starts with the sender's address (but not the name). Sometimes the address will be on the letterhead; otherwise it should be the first part. Next should be the date the letter was finished, written as month, day, and year. It should be two inches below the top and flush left (although some formats allow it to go in the center). Underneath that will be the inside address, or the recipient's address, including the specific name and title of the addressee, always left justified. The salutation is under that and should include the personal title unless it is someone usually referred to by the first name. The body is next. Block format is common and is single spaced and flushed left. There is a line between each paragraph. The content should be succinct, to the point, and logical. It might start with an opening and the main idea of the letter, followed with information supporting or explaining the main point. The final paragraph may reiterate the point and ask for action. Below that is the closing. If there are enclosures, this should be stated under that.

## Business memorandum format

A business memorandum is a relatively informal form of communication used in businesses to spread information, give announcements, explain company happenings, and provide similar functions. It is often sent out to a lot of people at once and does not generally contain confidential information. At the top it should state "Memorandum." Underneath that, flush left will be the word "TO:" along with the addressee(s). Underneath that and still flush left will be "FROM:" with the sender's name. If there are any CCs, this will be under that. Below that will be "DATE:" with the date. "SUBJECT:" is under that. Finally, the body of the memo will be underneath that, written in block format. A properly formatted memo is professional and succinct.

## Presentations

Goals
Presentations can have one or more goals, and it is important for presenters to be aware of the specific objectives so they can tailor the presentation for maximum efficacy. One major goal of presentations is to give information to the audience. It might be to employees, the stockholders, the public, or another group, but the company may be presenting information about itself, its products, current news, or more. Reporting data is another common goal of presentations. For instance, a company may be reporting sales numbers to its stockholders. Sometimes presentations are made to convince an audience of something. For example, a company may give a presentation to a potential client in an effort to broker a deal. Inspiring is another common goal. This is often done in employee meetings. For instance, a company may have a meeting to motivate its employees to work harder to reach certain goals. It is vital for the presentation to match its goals and audience for the best chance of success.

Features of successful presentations
Presentations play a big part in business, so it is important to know the features of successful ones. First, the audience should be able to understand the presentation. It needs to be tailored to the

audience so they can relate to it. It should be concise. The presenter should not carry on about the same thing because he (or she) could lose the audience. A good opening hook is important. It engages the audience from the start. Some people start with a story or quote. It should look good visually. Visual aids that can enhance a business presentation include graphs, charts, photographs, and videos. If the presentation contains a call to action, then it should be strong. The audience should be moved to do it. The presenter should be skilled. He should speak loud enough that everyone can hear, keep eye contact, and engage in good body language. He should appear confident. It should flow well and keep the audience's attention. Many business presentations are participative because this can keep people's interest. All of these measures go a long way in making a business presentation successful.

## Characteristics of various audiences

It is important for presenters to understand the characteristics of the audience for a business presentation because that can greatly influence the best presentation. The size of an audience matters. The presentation will be different for a small presentation of 10 people compared to a large presentation of 500. The cultural composition will matter. People of different cultures have different beliefs and may perceive a presentation differently. The other personal characteristics of the group, such as age, gender, and religion, can also affect how presentations are viewed. The level of knowledge matters. A health presentation on the same subject will be very different if given to a group of doctors as compared to a group of patients. Presenters should evaluate the audience to formulate the best presentation.

## Preparation steps

First, the presenter must understand his (or her) goals. What does he want to accomplish with the presentation? Once he knows this, he can select the exact topic, narrowing it down to fit the size and timing of the presentation. He will then need to evaluate the audience. The presentation of the same subject will be very different if given to customers as compared to employees or stockholders. The audience should be able to understand the topic, terminology, and references. The presenter should understand what is important to the audience and what they are thinking. Next, he should come up with the main points he wants to cover and make sure they are well illustrated in the presentation. He should find material to support these points such as graphs, charts, tables, photographs, data, and other visual items. This can give the presentation more substance and validity. Finally, the presenter should practice, ideally in front of someone who can evaluate the performance. By taking the time to carefully perfect the presentation, he will be more likely to reach his goals.

## Adjusting based on needs and concerns of audience

To make the most impact, a presenter should adjust his presentation based on the needs and concerns of the audience. First, he (or she) needs to understand the audience and how they will likely feel about the presentation. He should do as much research as possible into the characteristics of the audience, including whether they will accept the presentation with acceptance or hostility. He should plan to address their concerns. For instance, if he thinks the audience might be potentially hostile, he should right away include things that will help to alleviate their concerns or ease the news to them. He should explain things so that they understand and will hopefully accept the content. It is important for the presenter to show empathy to the audience so they feel like he is on their side. Oftentimes, the presenter allows the audience to ask questions and participate so that he can address their concerns directly. If they are worried about something that will not happen, then he should be reassuring. He should be personable and friendly. The more the presenter comes off as a caring and competent individual, the better the presentation will proceed.

## Delivery strategies

Different strategies can make presentation delivery more effective. One decision is whether to use an extemporaneous (unscripted) speech or a scripted one. If the person is knowledgeable enough and wants to engage the audience without looking at a paper or prompter, he (or she) might choose the unscripted version. If he thinks he would be too nervous or forgetful without it, he might choose to use a script. Anyone might need it for a very technical speech with a lot of statistics. No matter what, it is important for the presenter to display only positive body language. He should make eye contact with members of the audience and not just look down. He should use positive gestures, facial expressions, and enthusiasm. He should watch his words to make sure nothing can be interpreted as biased or inappropriate. It is important for the presenter to be aware of the audience at all times and respond as necessary. If he senses that they do not understand something, for instance, he should go into more detail. If they are upset about something, he should try to address their concerns. With the right strategies, the presentation has a greater chance of success.

## Visual aids

Visual aids can enhance a business presentation. Graphs and charts can give a visual representation of the subject. For instance, if a person is talking about how sales numbers have changed, a line graph can make this very clear by showing how sales have changed over time or in response to certain variables. Diagrams can give a visual explanation of a concept. Especially if something is technical, it can make it easier to understand. For instance, if someone is explaining a new product to investors, a diagram can help explain the product. Slideshows are commonly used in business presentations. They can reinforce what the presenter is saying and draw interest. If a company is talking about its charity work, a picture of a smiling child the company helped would be more compelling than just talking about it. Videos can also show people a great deal. For instance, a company can make a video showing its factories or a new design. Computer projections are used as well. Most presentations use one or more visual aids.

## Whiteboards, presentation software, and multimedia equipment

Whiteboards are often used in presentations. These are dry erase boards that the presenter can write on. This is good because the presenter can write as he is speaking. This is also useful for a participative presentation in which the presenter asks the audience a question and writes down the answers as they are given. He can show step-by-step how something is done. Presentation software is very commonly used. PowerPoint is one of the most commonly used presentation software programs and allows presenters to create detailed slides of photographs, charts, graphs, and more to enhance the presentation. They can make it easier to understand numbers and statistics. There are also various types of multimedia equipment a presenter might use. They might use a projector or a television. All of these can catch the audience's attention and bring the presentation to life.

## Telecommunication modalities used in business

The telephone is one form of telecommunication modalities. Individuals can get immediate access to someone to ask a question or have a discussion. A disadvantage is that there is no record of it (unless the call is recorded) and someone may not be available for a phone call. Another common form is a fax machine. This allows someone else to see a document. It is almost immediate. Both locations must have faxing ability, and it creates a physical document instead of a digital record, which many businesses prefer. Videoconferencing is commonly used. Individuals can discuss matters in real time. They can also share charts, graphs, and other visual aids. It has lowered the need for many business trips. Network email is also commonly used in business. It is delivered almost immediately and leaves a record. It can take longer to explain something than a simple phone conversation, however. An advantage is that it can be less intrusive and sometimes quicker.

## Internet modalities used in business

Email can be used to communicate with other businesses and with customers. Many customers prefer to email a company and it can be less time consuming for the company than a phone call. People like the convenience of being able to do it at any time. Message boards are also used. This is advantageous because customers can look up threads with topics similar to their issues and might get the answer to the problem without needing to contact customer service themselves. Listservs allow businesses to send out emails to many people at once. It is a great way for a company to disseminate information. Many companies also have instant messaging, both between its employees and for customers. This can be a great way to give customer service because customers like getting answers right away. One employee can be on several chats at once, which lowers the amount of employees needed as compared to phone support. Chat rooms are also convenient because multiple people can see the answers. Many businesses use a combination of these.

## Communication technologies used in business

Cell phones are very commonly used. These are advantageous because people can take them while they're on the go and be reachable even when not sitting at a desk in the office. Of course, they do not always get service everywhere. Fax machines are used to communicate a document over long distances. They are almost instantaneous, inexpensive, and create a hard copy. Bluetooth is a wireless technology that provides convenience by letting data travel over short distances. It has lowered the need for wires. Streaming technology has allowed multimedia to be constantly delivered and received from one party to another. For instance, a person can watch a live newscast on a phone. Voice over Internet Protocol (VoIP) allows voice and multimedia to go over the Internet and other Internet Protocol Networks (IP). An example is Skype. It is advantageous for businesses because it is inexpensive and offers high bandwidth efficiency. Because voice and data communications can use one network, infrastructure costs are lower. In addition, it can be run on inexpensive standard interfaces like personal computers. It can be less reliable, however.

## Etiquette in electronic communications

It is important to use professionalism in electronic communications, especially if it is a business letter. Just because it is sent via email does not mean it should be sloppy. Of course, how professional it is will depend on the recipient, but if it is to a professional contact, it should be formed professionally. They shouldn't use all capitals. They should make a proper introduction and closing and avoid emoticons. It is very important to make sure it is free of typos and grammatical errors. Senders should proofread it just as they would proofread a regular letter. It is also important to not bombard people with unnecessary emails. Senders should be careful about including someone in a chain of unnecessary emails. They should make use of BCC and not share people's addresses with others. They should write an appropriate subject line so people know what it is. Senders should be careful about confidential information because users can easily forward them. By following these rules, the email will be more professional.

# Economics

## Microeconomics

Microeconomics is one of the major parts of economics. It looks at how individuals and small organizations act and make decisions. It looks at the buyers and sellers and how their decisions affect supply and demand, price, and output. It also looks at how they decide their level of output and how much to charge for their products. It covers many different elements such as decision making with limited resources, market failure, and perfect competition. It looks at preference relations, and the choices people can make. It looks at supply and demand to see what affects them and how equilibrium can be reached. It also covers elasticity, consumer demand theory, theory and costs of production, and the types of markets such as perfect competition and monopolies. Additional topics include game theory, labor economics, economies of information, and welfare economics. Opportunity costs are also examined.

## Elasticity

Elasticity refers to how one variable changes in response to another. It describes how consumers respond when something changes. For instance, if the price of a product changes, will the demand change a lot or a little? The price elasticity of demand can be calculated with the equation:

Price Elasticity of Demand = (% Change in the quantity demanded) / (% Change in the price)

For instance, if the price of a good goes up by 50 percent and the quantity demanded goes down by 10 percent, then the price elasticity would be -10% / 50%, or 0.2. (Technically there would be a negative sign, but this is usually discarded.) If the price elasticity is greater than one, then the demand is considered elastic. This means that there will be a greater change in quantity demanded than the percentage change in price. Thus a higher price will cause lower revenues, and a lower price can increase revenues. If the price elasticity is less than one then it is inelastic and a percentage change in price corresponds to a smaller percentage change in demanded quantity. Thus a higher price equals higher revenue. A price elasticity equal to one means price changes won't affect revenue.

## Scarcity

Scarcity refers to how there are limited resources for unlimited wants in people. This means resources must be carefully allocated because using them for one thing means giving up another. Resources that are scarce include land, labor, and capital. Scarcity can affect price. If something is scarce, then it can have higher prices. Scarcity can change—for instance, a crop may become less available due to weather conditions—and the price can vary with it. A good is considered scarce if there are fewer units available than the amount people want. Individuals and companies try to decide how best to allocate these limited resources for the maximum return.

## Factors of production

There are four main factors of production: land, labor, capital, and entrepreneurship. Land encompasses the natural resources used in the production of goods and services. Besides literal land, it also includes wood, farms, fisheries, metal, and other natural substances. Labor encompasses all human resources such as the workers in businesses with the exception of the entrepreneur. The entrepreneur is his (or her) own factor of production because it is his idea that will make the business happen. He uses the other resources to create a good or service that will be profitable. He accepts the risks and reaps the rewards and creates the business. The final factor of production is capital, which can be defined as either the money used to purchase the resources necessary for the business, or the large physical assets utilized in production such as vehicles, buildings, and equipment. These four factors of production can be combined to create a business.

## Diminishing returns

"Diminishing returns" refers to the concept that, as one factor of input is increased (while all others stay constant), eventually the marginal or incremental output will start to decrease. It is not that there will not be increased output (although at times this can occur) but that the incremental amount will not be as much. An example is giving plant food to plants. As a gardener gives the plants food, at first there will be an increase in the plants, but as more and more plant food is added, the difference will be less and less until there is no discernible difference. This law is true of many items as well as labor, and should be considered so that companies are not spending the resources to add an input that is not making a worthwhile difference in output.

## Economies of scale

With economies of scale, as the volume of output increases, it costs less per unit to produce it. This is true of a number of products, especially when overhead is high. For instance, a video game manufacturer might spend a lot of money to design, create, and program a video game. If they only make ten units of the game, the cost per unit would be very high. If instead they make 100,000 copies of the game, the cost of production per unit would be significantly less. This is true for products such as medications, which cost a lot to develop, but then may not cost a lot to produce.

## Economies of scope

"Economies of scope" is when it is cheaper to produce a range of products rather than just one. The company may be able to benefit from one function for both such as the same marketing department. A company that makes toys may use the same advertisements to advertise similar but not identical products. Other major departments such as IT may be the same as well. Also, the output of one might be used for another such as a company that produces chocolate chips and then also uses those to make chocolate chip cookies. Also, the company may be able to sell them near to each other such as a toy manufacturer that can sell the toys together.

## Impact of company size on cost of different factors of production

The size of a company can affect the cost of the different factors of production. For instance, a larger company may have more land or use more natural resources. Because they use so much, they may pay less for each unit; there is often a cheaper per-unit cost when things are bought in high numbers. Overall they may pay more if they use more land. A larger company may have less difficulty attracting employees. Employees may be willing to take a lower salary because of it. Of course, a bigger company will need more employees and some of these employees will be more skilled, higher-paid employees, which can increase the overall cost. A larger company is likely to need more in the way of capital and will therefore spend more money on that as well. Again, they may get pricing discounts, so it may be a lower per unit cost.

## Equilibrium

Equilibrium refers to when there are balanced economic forces. For a product, this is when demand is equal to supply. The spot where the demand curve and supply curve meet is where the equilibrium price is. The equilibrium price will not change on its own, but can change with the emergence of external factors. For instance, if consumer preferences change, then the demand might go down and thus the supply may rise. Due to this, a short time of disequilibrium might occur as the market adjusts. Subsequently, a new equilibrium price will emerge, and equilibrium will be reestablished. Equilibrium can also refer to other variables in economics. For instance, there may be an ideal interest rate for growth.

## Opportunity costs

Opportunity costs are what a company gives up by choosing a different path. For instance, if a company can make five laptops or five desktop computers with the same resources, and it chooses to make the laptops, then the opportunity cost will be the five desktops. When managers make decisions, they need to consider the opportunity costs of various paths to determine the best path. Sometimes what they give up may be more worthwhile than what they are making, and then they need to consider a path where they won't incur the opportunity cost. Opportunity costs help determine which party has a comparative advantage. For instance, if a company can make 10 shirts in one hour or 20 pants in one hour, then the opportunity cost of the 10 shirts is the 20 pants and the opportunity cost of the 20 pants is 10 shirts. It has a comparative advantage with the pants because it has a lower opportunity cost. The company that has the lowest opportunity cost for a product has a comparative advantage in that product. It makes sense to spend its resources making that product and purchase the other product elsewhere.

## Supply and demand

Supply is defined as how much of a good or service the market has to offer to buyers. Producers are willing to make a certain amount of a good and this is supply. The amount producers make varies based on many variables and is very much based on price. The law of supply states that the higher the price of a good, the more of it the producers are willing to make (with everything else being equal). If they will receive more money for a product, they will make more to increase their revenues. Demand is how much of a good or service buyers want. This also can vary due to price. The law of demand shows that the higher the price, the lower the demand (with everything else being equal). Buyers are willing to buy more of a product if it is cheaper. The supply and demand for a product or good can be shown in a graph by two intersecting lines.

## Key assumptions of microeconomics

One of the key assumptions of microeconomics is that individuals possess preferences. They may like brand A more than brand B. They also try to maximize their happiness while minimizing the cost. They try to get as much happiness for whatever they can. Another is that individuals must engage in competition for resources that are limited. Microeconomics assumes rational behavior. It assumes their decisions make logical sense. It also says that people try to get as much as they can for the money they have because they do not have an unlimited amount of money. These assumptions make it easier to apply the theories of microeconomics and account for complex human behaviors.

## Adam Smith's theories of microeconomics

Adam Smith (1723-1790) was a Scottish philosopher who is known as modern economics' founder. He created classical economics. He felt that, when people work in their own self-interest and get the products they need, that the market will self-regulate itself and produce the best outcome for all. Supply and demand will come together if the market is just left to its own devices. This is known as the invisible hand. He promoted laissez-faire policies and was a free-market capitalist. In 1776, he published *The Wealth of Nations,* which describes the self-regulation. Many economists used his theories as a springboard for their own work.

## Circular flow economic model

The circular flow economic model shows a simplified way of how money and products make their way through the economy. It divides the parties as households and firms and shows two distinct markets: goods and services markets and factor markets, which represent the market for the factors of production such as land, labor, and capital. The goods and services market shows the finished product moving from the firms to the market and then to the households while money moves from the households to the market to the firms. In the factors of production market, everything is reversed. The households are the "sellers"; for instance, they provide the labor. Thus the factors of production move from the households to the market and to the firms. The firms pay for this, so the money moves from the firms to the market to the households in this part of the model. The money then flows through the households and firms, leaving a sustainable economy.

## Factors that influence economic change

Individual wants can influence economic change, as do the choices people make. The production of goods influences it. When production rises or falls for different reasons, the economy will be affected. Of course, competition plays a large part in the economy. Scarcity, or when items are in short supply, also plays a part. Prices can go up when this happens. Consumption is defined as the purchase of goods and services and the amount of it will influence the economy as well. All of these factors combine to contribute to economic change.

## Influence of supply and demand on price of goods

Demand and supply affect the price of goods. The price is where supply equals demand on the demand curve. If demand goes up and supply stays the same, then the price will rise. More people will be competing for the same amount of products. Alternatively, if demand goes down and supply stays the same, then the price will go down because fewer people will want it. If supply goes up and demand stays the same, then the price will go down. There will be more products for the same demand. If supply goes down and demand stays the same, then the price will go up because there will be fewer products for the same demand. A high supply on a related product can affect both products. First, the higher supply on the related product will drive prices down for that related product. If the related product is a substitute (i.e., pens versus pencils) and the price has gone down, then buyers will move to that product and have less demand for the original product. When the demand goes down for the original product, the price will go down too. Thus both prices may go down.

## Marginal benefits, marginal costs, marginal utility, the law of diminishing returns, and optimization

Marginal benefits describe the utility or satisfaction an individual gets from one more unit of a service or good. It is how much they will pay for that extra unit. Oftentimes this amount will go down with more units. For instance, someone may be willing to pay five dollars for a hair bow, but once she has bought five bows, she would only pay four dollars for another. Marginal costs describe how much it costs to make one more unit of something. Companies may use it to find the best level of production. Marginal utility refers to the satisfaction a consumer will get from one more unit. This can be positive or negative. The law of diminishing returns refers to the fact that, as there is an increase in a factor of production (holding all other factors steady), eventually the per unit output of that factor will go down. For instance, if there is one cook in a busy kitchen, adding one more will make a big difference. Once you add 10 more cooks, however, then each additional one will not make as big a difference.

## Perfect competition

In the market structure of perfect competition, all companies make products that are exactly the same. They are identical, and because of this, no one firm has a large market share. The companies all have a small share. These firms do not have control over pricing. The buyers know the pricing for each firm as well as complete information regarding the product itself. There is complete freedom to enter or exit the market. Although there may be no one market that is exactly like this, some are close, including agriculture. There are a lot of buyers and sellers in perfect competition, and supply and demand drive prices. The profit earned is modest and allows them to just stay in business because more firms enter when it rises.

## Monopolistic competition

Monopolistic competition is characterized by a market with many different producers that sell similar, although not identical, products. It is a form of imperfect competition. They are not perfect substitutes because of their differences, but they are very similar. The differences may be in quality, branding, or another area. One example would be restaurants. There may be a hundred Italian restaurants in an area that all serve Italian food, but none of them serve the exact same products. The consumers understand this and will often make decisions based on factors other than price. There are often a lot of consumers, and no one business controls the pricing of the market. There are not a lot of barriers to entry, so many competitors can go into the market. They do have some market power and they make their own decisions without regard to the market, but they also have imperfect information.

## Oligopoly

An oligopoly occurs when there are only a small amount of businesses supplying a certain product, meaning there is very limited competition. At times, this occurs when companies collude together to reduce competition and gain the ability to charge higher prices for their products. Because there are so few competitors, companies are very aware of each other and will often make decisions based on the actions of the other companies. Sometimes the companies try to collude, although this is illegal in some places. A cartel occurs when this collusion is formalized. Some oligopolies do feature fierce competition, however, and prices can be lower for it. An example is the cellular phone market, which has several large firms controlling most of the market.

## Monopoly

A monopoly occurs when one company is the only provider of a product. Everyone who wants to receive that product or service must get it through the one entity. There is no competition and no reasonable substitute that consumers can purchase. Because the company is the only seller and does not have to compete, it can charge high prices for the product. If a consumer wants the product, he will have no choice but to pay whatever the company is asking. A government may make them or they may form on their own. Many countries such as the United States have laws that restrict monopolies to promote healthy competition.

## Effects of competition

Competition affects the behavior of individual firms. Individual firms that have to compete against others may be forced to lower their prices in order to stay competitive. They may also make decisions on location based on where competitors are located. For instance, they may strive to stay away from a very heavy competitor. With a lot of competition, consumers may get more of a choice of products and services. Each company may work hard to differentiate its product and make it unique to attract more of the market. The economy can also be very efficient in a market economy. Consumers can benefit greatly from healthy competition.

## Competitive strategies

There are different competitive strategies that businesses employ to gain a competitive advantage. With cost leadership, a company charges less for the product to attract more customers. With penetration pricing, a business offers a low cost initially to get customers and then slowly raises it. With economy pricing, it strives to offer the lowest cost through the most basic items. With skimming, the initial price is high, but then it goes down to compete. In bundle pricing, a variety of products are offered together. There are a wide variety of promotional pricing strategies such as percent off sales. There are many non-price competition strategies as well. One is differentiation, in which a company tries to produce a unique product. The differences may be real, or they may just appear to be there. They may offer features that are better or different than the competitors' products, or they may try to increase the quality of the product. For instance, a phone manufacturer will try to produce innovative or higher quality features. Some strategies involve analyzing the market and customizing the strategy to the different groups. These strategies may be used independently or in conjunction with each other.

## Macroeconomics

Macroeconomics is a major part of economics and looks at the entire economy. It looks at the structure, performance, and behavior of an economy, focusing on large scale factors such as employment, distribution of wealth, sustainability, national income, growth rate, gross domestic product, prices, and inflation. There are many models that look for the reasons behind national income fluctuations and factors behind economic growth, looking for ways to maximize income and economic growth. Popular theories include those of Milton Friedman and John Maynard Keynes, supply-side economics, and monetarism. It looks at regional, national, and even global economies. Economic policies often come from macroeconomic model forecasts.

## Economic indicators, aggregate supply and demand, deflation and inflation, and fiscal and monetary policy

Economic indicators are statistics that provide information about economic activity. It lets people evaluate economic performance and forecast the future based on it. It includes gross domestic product, the consumer price index, and bankruptcies. Aggregate supply and demand refers to the price level for the country as a whole and the total goods and services made by suppliers in the country. Deflation is when the general price of goods and services go down, while inflation is when it goes up. Fiscal policy is the government's use of spending and taxing to influence the economy. It must balance these two practices. Fiscal policy can have an effect on individual spending, interest rates, deficit levels, exchange rates, and more. Monetary policy can also lead to growth or slowing of the economy, but it is done through the Federal Reserve. They can influence with open market operations such as transactions with US government bonds. By changing reserve requirements, the supply of money can be changed. In addition, they can make changes by altering the discount rate.

## Effects of taxes on people, companies, and the economy

Tax cuts greatly affect people, companies, and the economy. If they are done in the right way, they can be stimulating to the economy. With reduced taxes, people may spend more. If done incorrectly, it can cut the ability of the government to spend too much, which can be a significant problem for governments and citizens. Taxes can be progressive, which means people earning lower incomes pay a lower percentage. This is how the income tax system is in America. This allows the lower income people to keep more of their money, and the higher income people who have more to spare give a greater proportion. A regressive tax is the opposite – those who make less pay a higher percentage. With a proportional or flat tax, everyone pays the same percentage no matter what they make. Taxes are a common source of discussion and dissention in the government.

## Theories of economics

There are many different theories of economics. John Maynard Keynes (1883-1946) was an economist who helped create modern macroeconomics. He promoted government financial intervention to calm the results of the expansion and contraction phases of the business cycle. Milton Friedman thought people consumed an amount based on permanent income. He advocated free markets and thought government intervention should be reduced. Monetarism is a theory surrounding the government controlling the quantity of money in a market. It asserts that inflation is dependent upon the amount of money printed. Milton Friedman thought this amount should be relatively level. Supply-side economics, also known as "Reaganomics," is the trickle-down policy. It states that giving tax cuts for entrepreneurs and investors will allow them to invest more and give economic benefits to everyone through a trickle-down idea. The three pillars it stands on are regulatory policy, tax policy, and monetary policy, and it asserts that supply is the most vital element to economic growth. All of these theories have both proponents and opponents.

## Major economic systems

There are various economic systems, including traditional, market, command, and mixed. A traditional market system is, as the name suggests, based on tradition. They make products because of customers, beliefs, etc. Many of these are in developing countries. A command economic system is one in which the government controls a great deal of the economic system. They may regulate resources or own everything. A market economic system is like a free market. Organizations are run by the people, and they shape the market, not the government. In a mixed economic system, the command and market system are combined. This is very common and can vary in the combination. The free market does a lot, but the government will control some things such as preventing monopolies. This is seen in the United States, as well as many other developed nations.

## Open and closed economies

A closed economy is one that is wholly self-sufficient. There is no international trading of any kind, no exporting, and no importing. There is no investment in other countries, either by the country or by others into the country with the closed economy. Everything produced within the country is sold and used within that country. An open economy is the opposite of a closed economy. The people and businesses may export and import goods and services as well as exchange technology. Citizens can invest in projects in foreign countries and the country accepts investments from those outside of the country. This is advantageous in that the people can enjoy products and services from many countries, giving them a larger selection. It also gives them the opportunity to invest in other countries as well as an outlet to export items.

## Capitalist, communist, and socialist economies

A capitalist economy allows for private ownership and a free market. Supply and demand drive the market, and individuals can own businesses and personally enjoy the profits. Supply and demand keep prices in check. There is free competition without government interference. In communism, everything is owned communally. The point is to eliminate the gap between the wealthy and the poor with everyone owning everything and everyone seeing the benefits. In socialism, most of the production is run through the government for the benefit of all, although there can be some ownership of private property. There should be less of a gap between the wealthy and poor, although not a completely nonexistent one. The government should work to redistribute wealth to promote fairness. Most economies are not purely one of these but a combination of two or more.

## Business cycle

The business cycle describes the changes in the economy. These include production, trade, and the economy in general. Expansion is a time when production and pricing are being increased. Interest rates and unemployment are low while the GDP is higher. Some theorists feel that government spending should be less at this time. The peak is when this gets the highest. Contraction is a time when the opposite is happening. Production and the GDP are going down while unemployment is going up. Some feel that the government should be spending more at this time to stimulate the economy. When it gets to its lowest, it reaches the trough.

## Inflation

Inflation is the increase in prices that leads to a lowering of dollar value as time passes. Many economies experience about two to three percent inflation a year. If the inflation rate is three percent, for instance, then a candy bar that costs $1.00 at the beginning of the year will cost $1.03 at the end. Hyperinflation occurs when inflation is extremely high. This is very rare and can be disastrous for an economy. Stagflation is when high inflation occurs at the same time as stagnation in the economy. The opposite of inflation is deflation, in which prices decrease. Inflation is caused by various factors. Demand-pull inflation occurs when demand is increasing at a higher rate than supply, so prices go up. Growing economies might see this. In cost-push inflation, companies have higher costs and increase prices so their profit margins do not go down. Inflation can show growth in the economy and lack of it can show a weakening economy. Anticipated inflation is not usually a big deal, but unanticipated inflation can hurt the economy. For instance, uncertainty might mean people don't spend as much and the country might not be as competitive as other countries.

## Unemployment

Unemployment occurs when people are actively looking for work but are unable to find it. There is always some unemployment, but the number varies. When there is a lot of economic growth and the economy is in a state of expansion, unemployment is lower; alternatively, when it is in a decline, unemployment is higher. There are different types of unemployment. Structural unemployment occurs when the labor market has inefficiencies. There will be structural economic issues. For instance, the skills needed for the jobs and the skills of the workers might not match. This might occur when the technological needs of jobs increase and the workers do not have this know-how. Frictional unemployment happens when a worker is moving between jobs. The worker might not have the information or the skills for the new job or may not get a good offer. Cyclical unemployment is due to contractions in the economy. For instance, if there is a recession, the job openings will go down. Seasonal unemployment is expected because of the time of year. For instance, there may be fewer employees at a ski resort in the summer.

## Gross national product

The gross national product is comprised of the market value of everything produced by a nation's citizens in a one-year period. It is whatever goods and services are produced by one people. It does not matter where it is produced, but instead who produces it. Thus for the United States, it would include all products and services produced by Americans, both in the United States and abroad. It does not include items produced in the United States by foreign entities. It is calculated by taking the market value of the production in a country, adding the market value of goods and services produced by the people of that country in foreign areas, and subtracting the value of items produced by foreigners. The number can aid in government policy making as well as business decision making. It can also be used in the evaluation of economic theories. It can give an idea of the health of an economy.

## Gross domestic product

The gross domestic product describes the value of goods and services produced within a country, typically annually. It is calculated by adding consumer spending (private consumption) within a country, spending by the government, capital spending, and net exports (exports minus imports). This is called the expenditure approach. It can also be calculated with a production approach and income approach. It does not matter who owns the products or services, only that it occurs within the country. It is used to evaluate the health of an economy, especially growth. It can give an idea of whether a recession is occurring and what the results of an economic policy are. It can affect the stock market and will often signal other things such as unemployment and wages.

## Consumer price index and producer price index

The consumer price index (CPI) looks at the weighted mean of prices of a basket of goods or services to see how the price changes. To calculate it, the prices of a variety of representative items are gathered for a period of time. The price changes for each item are averaged, and the items are weighted based on how important they are. This calculation can show changes in the cost of living as well as deflation and inflation. The equation for one item is current CPI = item price × price in base year × (current CPI / base-year CPI). It is not perfectly accurate in estimating the cost of living. The producer price index (PPI) calculates the mean difference in selling prices domestic producers get over a period of time. The areas of production it considers are commodity-based, industry-based, and stage-of-processing-based companies. The PPI is often used because it can help predict the CPI.

## Index of leading economic indicators

The index of leading economic indicators is used to forecast the economy in future months. There are a variety of components used in its calculation. These include the following: manufacturing employees' weekly hours, unemployment insurance applications, orders going in to manufacturers for goods and materials for consumers, how quickly merchandise travels from vendors to suppliers, capital goods' new orders (not defense), residential buildings' new building permits, S&P 500 stock index, monetary supply adjusted for inflation, the difference between short interest rates and long interest rates, and the sentiment of consumers. These indicators can give an idea of where the economy is headed. Firms and investors look at it when making business decisions.

## Rate of unemployment

The United States regularly calculates the rate of unemployment. To calculate unemployment, the government administers a survey every month called the Current Population Survey (CPS). These may be in person or on the phone. Census Bureau interviewers look at 60,000 households in a sample to replicate the United States. They ask about employment and find the percentage that is unemployed. Unemployed is classified as people who are not working, have been searching for work in the past four weeks, and are able and available to get a job. Interviewers also look at other statistics such as the characteristics of the unemployed workers. The rate of unemployment can give an overall view of the economy and help shape policies. Unemployment is important because, when people are unemployed, the nation does not have the products or goods the worker would have made. Also, there is lowered purchasing power, and other workers may become unemployed because of it. The government will look at the statistics surrounding unemployment to make policy decisions that affect the economy and unemployment.

## Rate of inflation

Inflation is how much goods and services increase in price as time changes. To calculate inflation, a price index such as the consumer price index may be used. This shows the prices of goods and services for an average person. The government uses this to measure how prices change over a year. The following equation is used:

Inflation = ((current year price index – base year price index) × 100) / base year price index.

For instance, if the price index went from $100 to $110 the next year, then the equation would be ((110 - 100) × 100) / 100, or 10 percent inflation. This can be negative if prices went down—this would be called deflation. There are other price indices that can be used such as the commodity price index, cost of living index, and producer price index. Policymakers use the rates of inflation to make decisions. For instance, a government may change its monetary policy to influence inflation. This may involve changing interest rates or creating wage controls.

## Federal Reserve System

Formed in 1913, the Federal Reserve System is the United States' central banking system. It works to keep employment up, keep prices stable, and moderate interest rates in the long term. It also works with monetary policy, oversees banks, keeps the United States financial system stable, performs research, and provides financial services. It can help in a time of financial crisis or panic. It helps keep the balance between banking and government. It is the bank of the government and of other banks. It can act as a lender of last resort as well. It provides many payment services and also works to provide an elastic currency. Its policies and work provide many functions to the banking system.

## Government fiscal policies that can affect the economy

Tax policy makes a large difference. There is a lot of debate on exactly how taxes affect the economy, but in some cases, a reduction in taxes may cause people to spend more and can stimulate the economy. Of course, there will be less money for the government to spend, which can also affect the economy. Another factor that can affect the economy is government bond sales. Bonds make a difference because they help to determine interest rates, and therefore liquidity. Interest rates affect how easily people can buy things. Government price controls are when governments limit the price of a good or service in an attempt to keep the items affordable. Price ceilings and price floors are two examples. There is debate on how effective these are. All of these factors combine to affect the economy.

## Interest rates

In general, an interest rate is the percentage of interest charged by a lender to a borrower. Essentially it is what it costs to borrow money. A fixed interest rate stays the same for the length of the loan, while a variable interest rate can vary as the market rates change. The annual percentage rate (APR) is the percentage of interest for a loan based annually. This is often used for credit cards and makes it easier to compare various credit cards to each other. The prime rate is the benchmark rate of interest, which banks often use when calculating rates for loans. This is used in the United States. A teaser rate may be a special, limited time rate that is offered to attract people.

# Entrepreneurship

**Effects of entrepreneurs on business and the economy**

Entrepreneurs can drive innovation. Entrepreneurs come up with new ideas that haven't been thought of before. In a large company, it can be difficult to get a new idea across with so many layers, but an entrepreneur has no such limits. Entrepreneurs also create jobs, both for themselves and the employees they hire. People who have difficulty finding a job may start a company on their own. They also fill niches. Entrepreneurs might see places where there is an unfulfilled need through their own or others' experiences. They can make a product or service to fill this need. At times, more established companies have to make changes to respond to entrepreneurs. Entrepreneurs play a large part in the economy and can make a significant difference.

**Entrepreneurial opportunities due to changes and development in social, technological, and economic factors**

Changes in social, technological and economic factors can provide entrepreneurial opportunities. Technology has made it easy for people to start a home-based business without a lot of capital. For instance, someone who makes products at home can sell them on the Internet and not have to open an actual store. It is also much less expensive to advertise if entrepreneurs take advantage of resources such as social media websites like Facebook and Twitter, where they can reach a lot of people without spending a lot of money. Home-based entrepreneurs can even sell internationally thanks to the Internet. With this lowered cost of entry, many entrepreneurs are forming startups. There is also more funding available to startups. In many societies, innovation and hard work are prized, and this can spur entrepreneurs. Many people are looking to fulfill their dreams of owning a business. Some may be having difficulty at regular jobs and want to be their own boss. Now that it's easier than ever, this is becoming a reality for many.

**Established and entrepreneurial ventures**

There are many differences between established and entrepreneurial ventures. An established firm might have a lot of money and a lot of customers. An entrepreneurial venture that is just starting out might be lacking in both. Oftentimes it can be difficult to bring new innovations in an established business. There might be many levels to go through, and the business may be set in its ways. An entrepreneurial venture can try new things more easily, and be more flexible. They may be more willing to take a risk or to use new channels. With less money, they may need to be more creative in their business such as by using social media to position themselves. Of course, there is much risk in entrepreneurial ventures, but many do stick around to become established businesses.

**Methods to compete with businesses**

It can be difficult for entrepreneurs to compete with established businesses, but a number of strategies can make a difference. First, they can try to differentiate their products so consumers will choose them. They can make their products stand out. They may offer excellent and personalized quality and service that people will appreciate. They also can use innovative and yet low cost methods to promote their products. For instance, many small companies became very successful using social media websites like Facebook and Twitter. They can promote their products with very little cost output. They can also use innovative ideas to promote brand loyalty such as a loyalty discount or club. Some companies will offer something for free such as a website that has a free and a premium service. An entrepreneur might offer a range of products for a wider market. He should get to know his audience well to entice them. It is also important for entrepreneurs to make sure their companies are healthy internally.

## Qualities of successful entrepreneurs

Successful entrepreneurs are typically good leaders. They are not afraid to lead others and can do so effectively. They have good interpersonal skills. They are very motivated and enthusiastic. They are usually hard workers willing to put in the time and effort to make their business a success. They are good at planning. Many new businesses fail, and this is often due to lack of a solid business plan. Successful entrepreneurs are generally organized and create good plans that account for contingencies, and can be flexible for times when things don't go according to plan. Successful entrepreneurs are thorough, meticulous, persistent, and do their research into the market and competitors. They are also good at managing money and promoting themselves and their businesses. They are passionate and willing to take risks. They have a vision and believe in themselves and their business.

## Benefits and drawbacks of entrepreneurship

There are both advantages and disadvantages to entrepreneurship. One advantage is that an entrepreneur can be his own boss. He will be able to control his working conditions such as location, time, and hours. Entrepreneurs often work from home, especially when starting a new business. He can make all of the business decisions. Also, he will enjoy all the success of the business. If the business makes millions, he might become a millionaire as compared to someone who works for a company and just makes a salary no matter how well the firm does. The disadvantages to entrepreneurship are also significant. The entrepreneur assumes all the risk. If the company fails, the entrepreneur can lose a great deal of money. Also, entrepreneurship typically involves hard work and long hours. He might have to make decisions without help. It can be a great deal of stress. It also often costs a lot of money (or the ability to raise a lot of capital) to start a business. A significant number fail in the first year, which can be very stressful, especially for someone who needs a secure form of income for a home, family, or other responsibilities.

## Benefits and drawbacks of starting business from home

With the advent of the Internet, starting a business from home is easier than ever before, yet it is still wrought with challenges. There are both benefits and drawbacks to home-based businesses. One benefit of a home-based business is the ability to work from the comfort of home. Entrepreneurs can enjoy their own personal environment. Also, some people have other responsibilities that preclude them from a job outside the home such as a stay-at-home mother. Entrepreneurs can save a significant amount of time and money with a home-based business. There is no commute, no gas money, and no need to rent an office. Entrepreneurs can also save money on taxes with business deductions. Entrepreneurs must consider the drawbacks of a home-based business. Many people find it difficult to work at home; distractions such as the computer or phone may keep them from realizing the efficiency they'd see in an office. Also, a home-based business can be difficult if the entrepreneur needs a professional place to meet with clients. They might not have room for an office or a place to store products. Also, some have restrictions on where a commercial venture can be located.

## Sole proprietorship

A sole proprietorship is a simple and common form of business ownership in which an individual starts an unincorporated business. Everything with the business is connected to the individual, therefore he (or she) is responsible for all debts and liabilities. If there is a problem, he could be personally liable. He also enjoys the profits from the business. It is not nearly as difficult or complex to start a sole proprietorship as many other types of businesses; although one must get the necessary licenses and follow regulations, it is not as complex as incorporating a business. Also, taxes are simpler because the taxes for the business are combined on the individual's personal income taxes, as opposed to having taxes just for the business. With a sole proprietorship, the individual has all control of the business and makes all of the decisions.

### Benefits and drawbacks
One advantage of a sole proprietorship is that the person has complete control over the company. He can make changes as he wishes and sell the company if he desires. There aren't any corporate taxes, and the legal costs and requirements are fewer and less complicated than when forming a corporation. Also, the sole proprietor will enjoy all of the profits and benefits of the company. A disadvantage is that the person may find it more difficult to find investors. He can also be legally liable for all the debts and any issues that occur because of the company or its employees. It can be challenging and a lot of work to be the sole proprietor and have to make all the decisions. If the company loses, so will the entrepreneur. Entrepreneurs should look at the pros and cons to decide whether a sole proprietorship is right for them.

## Partnerships

A partnership is formed when two or more individuals band together to form a business in which they share in the work, profits, liabilities, and other features of the business. It may be a general partnership, in which all partners share everything equally; a joint venture, which is similar to a general partnership, but which is temporary and encompassing a single project; or a limited partnership, in which a partner can have both limited liability and limited input into the business. Partnerships are registered with the state and must obtain required licenses and follow regulations. They are a generally easy type of business to form. Taxes must be filed specifically for the business, including annual return of income, excise taxes, and employment taxes. The partners are personally liable for the actions of the business as well as responsible for the debts. They share the profits, and partners can benefit from the expertise of each other. They all contribute to the business as well as the decision making. Partnerships are a common form of business.

### Benefits and drawbacks
There are both benefits and drawbacks to being in a partnership. One advantage is that the partners can bring different skills and qualities to the business. For instance, one partner might be great at creating a product but terrible at selling it, while the other might be a great salesperson. They can each complement one another. It takes the burden off of one person as far as the workload and decision making. In addition, it might be easier for the partners to share the cost and liabilities of the business. One person might not be able to afford to do it on his (or her) own. It is generally an easy type of business to form and relatively inexpensive. A business that lets employees become partners might find the employees are much more motivated. A disadvantage is that the partners might not agree on something and this can lead to adversity within the business. Also, the partners still have the liability of the business tied to them personally, including the decisions made by others in the business. Additionally, unlike sole proprietors, partners have to share their profits.

## Corporation

A corporation is a type of business that is its own legal entity, although it is owned by shareholders. The liabilities and debts are incurred by the corporation, not by the shareholders. They can raise money by selling stock so that investors can own a small part of the company. It is a complex form of business structure and requires administrative fees and complicated taxes. Usually corporations are bigger companies with numerous employees. They are formed when a party chooses a name and files forms to incorporate the business through the Secretary of State's office. There are various taxes that must be paid, including income taxes. This is a common form of business for larger businesses in the United States.

Benefits and drawbacks
One benefit of operating a corporation is that the shareholders are shielded from the debts and liabilities of the corporation. In other types of business such as a sole proprietorship, an owner could be legally liable based on the actions of the company. A corporation provides protection against this. Corporations also have the ability to gain funds by selling shares, or small portions of ownership in the company. Some of the profits may be taxed at a corporate rate, which is typically lower than the tax rate for individuals. Corporations also can often get better employees because of their size, benefits, and stock options. One disadvantage of a corporation is that it generally costs a lot more to start than other types of business. It can also take a lot more time and effort as it is more complicated and there is more paperwork. In some cases, profits can be double taxed when they are taxed both as income for the business and as personal income when shareholders receive dividends.

## Franchise

When someone owns a franchise, they pay a company for the right to recreate their business. They typically use the same name, products, style, and look. They also enjoy benefits from the advertising. They usually have very limited control; the company will dictate what the franchise owner can and cannot change. Customers expect a certain experience when they go to the store or restaurant, so it should be as uniform as possible. The person who owns the franchise can get the benefits of using an already proven brand with proven products that have a built-in customer base. An example is McDonald's.

Benefits and drawbacks
There are both benefits and drawbacks to owning a franchise. One advantage is that much of the hard work is already done. The company that owns the brand has already created a successful brand, product, look, etc. It can be very difficult to come up with all of these details. Another advantage is that there is a built-in audience of customers. For instance, people will seek out McDonald's because they know what to expect. This is different from starting a new business in which an owner has to convince consumers to give him (or her) a chance. One disadvantage of a franchise is that it costs money. Some of the profits will go to the franchise owner. Another disadvantage is the lack of control. Even if someone owns a franchise, he can't just make whatever changes he wants. He might not be able to change much of anything, which might be frustrating to some owners. Entrepreneurs should balance the pros and cons to decide whether a franchise is right for them.

## Variation of taxation between business ownership types

The taxation of a business will vary greatly depending on the type of business ownership. In a sole proprietorship, there is no separate tax filing for the business. Instead, the taxes related to the business are absorbed into the owner's individual tax filing. Business earnings would just be reported as income. A partnership is taxed in much the same way as a sole proprietorship, except it is divided between the individual partners who will then include it in their returns. A corporation is considered a separate taxable entity, however, and will be taxed as such. A tax filing must be done for the company, and it will be subject to a corporate income tax rate. Any owners that receive dividends will also pay personal taxes on those.

## Launching small businesses

The first step in launching a small business is to come up with a solid business plan. This should include every part of the business such as a description of the offerings, who is going to be involved, the target market, pricing, promotions, the financial plan, and more. If possible, the person should consider getting business counseling or training from a source such as the Small Business Administration. Next, the entrepreneur should consider a location for his business—somewhere where it will get noticed and attract customers. Next, the person has to get financing for the business. This can be in different forms such as a loan or capital investment. The entrepreneur then needs to follow all the procedures for a business of his type such as registering the name, setting up taxes, and attaining required licenses and permits. The more attention he pays to each step, the more likely he will be successful.

### Financing

One type of financing is through a loan. Some very beneficial loans are available through the Small Business Administration (SBA). They offer a loan called the 7(a) guarantee small business loan and another that is the 504 fixed-asset small business finance program. Various banks also offer similar loans. A small business may also try to attract a venture capitalist who invests in promising businesses. They typically want their money back relatively swiftly, but can give management experience. A capital investment may be done by banks, angel investors, equity investors, or financial institutions. Usually, common or preferred equity is issued, but there could also be straight or convertible debt. Small businesses can also finance their company through other means such as through loans from family and friends.

### Obstacles

It can be very difficult to get capital to start the business, especially if it is being started as a sole proprietorship. Lenders may not be willing to risk the money and thus the entrepreneur will have to work hard to finance the project. They must also be able to manage the money so it lasts until the business becomes profitable, which can take time even for a well-thought out business that will eventually succeed. Entrepreneurs must come up with a solid business plan and all the different aspects of their business, which means a lot of hard work, long hours, and perseverance. They must accept the risk; even good products and businesses may fail through no fault of the entrepreneur. They must find a way to make themselves stand out so people will choose them. There is a lot of competition in today's market, especially with how the Internet and technology has eased the ability to start a business, and entrepreneurs must contend with that.

# SBA

The Small Business Administration (SBA) was started by Congress in 1953 with the goal of aiding small businesses and the entrepreneurs starting them. They provide a wide variety of functions, including giving loans, grants, and loan guarantees. They also offer counseling and information to small businesses. The counseling is both across the Internet and in person at one of their many offices. On their website, entrepreneurs can learn about how to start a business, including important information such as securing financing. They also help people with government contracting and advocate for small businesses with the legislature. They conduct research, as well. They have local and larger offices to meet the needs of people.

## Factors that influence success of small businesses

There are various factors that influence whether a small business succeeds. First, the company has to be competitive and attract consumers. This might be through differentiation or providing better quality, value, or services. The company has to be able to secure stable financing. Depending on the business, it can cost a lot of money to start, and the company needs to make sure it has enough to see it through the beginning stages. Some companies that will eventually turn a profit fail to do so at the beginning. The location makes a big difference in whether a business succeeds. A restaurant in a busy shopping plaza will have a lot more exposure than one in a small and quiet strip mall. It's important for entrepreneurs to carefully choose the location of the business. Marketing decisions also make a large difference in whether the business succeeds. Companies that are very successful at marketing their business will attract more customers. They need to do a good job of retaining their customers, as well.

## Business plan

A business plan should be thorough and contain the necessary components to give the business the best chance of success. First, the business plan should provide a vision. This might be in the executive summary and show what the entrepreneur envisions his business will become. The plan should have a detailed description of the business, including the product, pricing, distribution, what makes it unique, and how it will gain a competitive advantage. It should discuss the background of the company, as well as the complete management team and key players. It needs to discuss the financial details of the company and should include a cash flow statement and projections of revenue. It should discuss the capital the company needs to start up, as well as give a detailed financial plan for the company that shows how profit will be made. A marketing plan also needs to be included. The target market should be clearly identified, as should a plan for marketing and advertising to them. A SWOT analysis should be conducted. A summary should wrap everything up at the end.

### Strategies

A solid business plan can make a large difference in whether a business succeeds. Different strategies can help an entrepreneur create such a plan. First, the person might want to seek help. For instance, the Small Business Administration gives counseling and also has information on making a business plan. The plan should be as thorough as possible, planning for as many contingencies and details as possible, but also flexible. It should give detailed numbers. The entrepreneur should perform as much research as possible. For instance, to attract investors, he (or she) may need to show exactly how he found his target market and how he is going to earn profits. He can show the investors that he "did his homework" and expects a certain return based not on wishful thinking, but on solid research and numbers. Entrepreneurs can also look at other successful business plans to help create their own.

# Information Technology

## Effects of computers and technology on business

One major way computers and technology have affected business is through communication. The Internet has made sending communication easy, inexpensive, and convenient, even if the recipient is on the other side of the world. People can send messages instantaneously and have conference calls with people in all areas, eliminating the need for business trips in some cases. It is also easy to send and access data from different areas, saving a great deal of money and time. Data can also be recorded, edited, and evaluated in many different ways, providing a wealth of information to businesses. Companies have new ways to promote and advertise their products; many of these, such as social media, are relatively inexpensive and powerful. Through the ease of the Internet, many smaller businesses can now compete with large businesses. Streaming video lets consumers get information immediately, and wireless technology makes it easier and more convenient. Computers and technology have benefited businesses tremendously.

## Effects of Internet on traditional media industries

The Internet has impacted traditional media industries in a number of ways. First, many people wish to view their news up-to-date on the Internet, and many news companies have opened extensive websites that are updated throughout the day as a response. They've had to keep up with the new speed of information brought by the Internet. Some of them have found new ways to earn money such as by requiring subscriptions to read online coverage. Many traditional newspapers have seen their readership decrease because of the information available on the Internet. They also have to compete with many more sources of information such as social media. Thus the Internet has provided both negatives such as increased competition, and positives such as new ways to reach people.

## Effects of computer technology on society

People can connect with each other across societies, cultures, and even oceans. It is easy and inexpensive to communicate with someone across the world with email or video. Some cultures have adopted new things from other cultures as a result. People can also express themselves in new ways. They can use it for art, make blogs, or create social media presences to share their views. Businesses have a much greater market to which to sell and can also more easily reach their target markets. It can also be less expensive to reach people through social media and other online options. Social networking in general is much easier. People can keep connected and share information very quickly. If a person or company can cause something to "go viral," it will reach many people. Businesses should take advantage of the new opportunities technology has provided.

## Effects of computer technology on politics

Political information can be quickly spread. A news headline does not have to wait for the evening news or tomorrow's newspaper to reach the public. Also, with social media, people can share political information, either positive or negative. They can try to influence their friends. If there is a major happening, it may go "viral" on social media, spreading the information within a matter of minutes. Political blogs have also popped up all over the Internet, where people can give their political opinions and try to inform (or sway) followers. Many politicians keep websites that they use to promote themselves. Computer technology has opened up a new door for political fundraising. It makes it easy for people to donate, even if it's just a few dollars. Those small contributions add up. The Internet has made quite a difference in the world of politics.

## Information technology needs of businesses

Companies should consider all the types of information technology that can help their company. First, they need a good system of data management. They need to maintain data on products, customers, and other business needs in a neat and organized fashion. There also should be a way to analyze the data. There are many programs that can accomplish this. Companies need technology for communications such as email capability. Many businesses do videoconferencing as well. Companies that perform e-commerce will need systems for that. Most large companies have a website, and many sell or promote their products on it. They need to have a system to take the orders efficiently and effectively. Some use technology for production. There are various other technology needs a company may have based on the industry.

## Steps in planning information technology

Companies should follow clear steps to plan their information technology to make sure they obtain the most effective, efficient, and cost-effective system. First, they need to evaluate their technology needs. They need to understand exactly what they need as far as technology in communication, production, accounting, and other functions. They should not just consider what they currently need, but what they might need as they grow. They should spend the time to research the trends in technology. There are always new things coming out in the technological field, and they want to take advantage of everything that is offered. They should then find someone who can design an information system that can address all of their needs. There are many companies that put together customized systems. They can get ready-made systems or get something personalized. The more they plan, the better system they will get.

## Strategies when acquiring information technologies

Companies need to be careful and logical when acquiring information technologies to ensure they receive the right products at the right prices. First, they need to evaluate both their current and future needs. They should consider the products they want and the functions provided. It is important for companies to look at competing products and services, evaluating them for features, quality, and support. They should research the different vendors and what they provide. Businesses will often purchase a great deal of equipment at one time and may get special deals or incentives. Some companies offer a bidding process in which they allow companies to bid for the contract. They will look at what each company offers at the price and choose the one that most aligns with their needs. By taking their time in this process, they will increase the chances of securing the best technology solutions.

## Bits, URLs, bytes, browsers, USB flash drives, bandwidth, and CD-ROM drives

In computing, a bit signifies the basic unit of information. It is generally 0 or 1. When bits are combined (usually in groups of eight) they make a byte. A URL stands for uniform resource locator and is the web address of a website. This will bring users to their desired website. A browser is the program most people use to navigate the Internet. Internet Explorer and Google Chrome are two common web browsers. USB flash drives are small portable drives that can be used to store information such as Word files. They can be connected to the USB ports on desktop computers, laptops, and other devices. Bandwidth is the bit-rate of resources of data communication. It describes the speed of the network. A CD-ROM drive can access, read, and play CDs.

## Basic computer parts

The system unit is where the main computing parts are located. It is often shaped as a tower and contains the central processing unit, which processes the information; and the random access memory, which temporarily houses information. It will typically contain drives such as a CD/DVD drive, a floppy disk drive, and a hard disk drive. Cables connect the other components to the main unit. A mouse allows the user to point to and select items. Some people use a track ball instead. A keyboard allows users to input information like letters, numbers, and characters. It has function keys, a numeric keyboard, and navigation keys. Users control the computer with its many functions. A monitor displays information in text and graphic form. A printer allows users to print documents as well as information from the screen. Speakers allow users to hear music, dialogue, and other sounds. A modem gives the user access to the Internet.

## Obtaining and evaluating Internet information

Those in business should be careful when obtaining and evaluating information from the Internet. There is a great deal of false information. Users should search for reputable websites such as websites of reliable news agencies, websites affiliated with schools, and well-known and trusted websites. Search engines are a powerful tool for finding information. Users should choose their keywords carefully. They may want to make use of quotation marks if searching for a particular phrase or use "+" or "-" if there is a word they want included in their search results or not. There are a number of other advanced search features such as a site search. Once a website is reached, users should determine its credibility by factors such as its author (although people will lie about their credentials); who it is affiliated with; if the information is up to date; and whether there are any biases such as if the person is trying to sell something. They can also confirm the information by looking on several websites.

## Utilization of Internet by businesses

One of the ways businesses use the Internet is it to communicate, both with business associates and with their customers. Many of them have an email system that facilitates that. Companies also communicate with their customers in other ways on the Internet such as through live chat or through social media websites like Facebook and Twitter. Many customers prefer to reach customer service through the Internet. The Internet is also very commonly used for promotion. It can be a very cost-effective way to reach many customers. For instance, many companies try to have a strong social media presence that allows them to reach a lot of people while only spending a small amount of time, effort, and money. The Internet can also be used in research. For instance, a company can learn about their competition or perform market research. Of course, many companies actually sell on the Internet, giving the convenience of anytime shopping from home to their customers. Companies should take advantage of all the Internet has to offer.

## Business uses of the web

Most companies offer websites, where business partners, clients, and customers can learn about what they offer. Oftentimes, items are sold directly through these websites. Customer service is also offered through websites. This makes it available 24/7. Blogs are also often seen on the Internet. People in companies write regular articles about the company or other subjects. This can keep people interested in the company. Companies also get email mailing lists so they can send out mass emails to customers. They can also take advantage of social media to promote their companies. Most companies use many of these strategies.

## Networks and networking

Many businesses possess computer networks that provide a wide variety of functions. A local area network (LAN) gives a group of nearby computers networking capability. For instance, they can share files, games, printers, and so forth. This can be inexpensive and easy to set up. They can be wired or wireless and can be connected to each other when networking needs grow. When it grows so large that it might go across cities or even countries, the company can make a wide area network (WAN) to connect their systems. The Internet itself is a WAN. The employees can usually go on the Internet from the network. A virtual private network (VPN) gives employees remote access to the network. The business can also have an intranet with internal web servers that let employees distribute confidential information to each other. This may include an internal email system as well as instant messaging and other forms of communication. To access this information, employees must be logged into the network. Many companies have a wide variety of computer systems.

## Security threats due to use of technology in business

Technology provides many useful applications for business, but there are also substantial security risks. Online fraud is one common threat, and comes in many forms. Someone might pretend to be someone else and convince an individual or business to share financial information. They may sell a nonexistent or defective item. Identity theft is also very common. Someone will steal a person's personal information and make purchases using his or her credit. A major threat for companies is getting their personal or business information hacked. Several major issues have arisen when customers' credit card information was stolen from major store chains. These numbers were then utilized in identity theft. There are a number of ways companies can lower this risk through the use of firewalls and other security measures, but they will always exist to some extent.

## Security measures when using technology

With the prevalence of identity theft, scams, and online fraud, it is important for businesses to protect themselves when using technology. One measure is to use password protection. Access to sensitive information should be protected by passwords. These passwords should not be easy to crack and should never be shared. In some cases, there should be multiple passwords. Businesses also encrypt their information. This is where the messages are encoded or changed so they can only be read by the correct users. Even if someone intercepts the message, he (or she) will not be able to interpret it. Another strategy is the use of firewalls. These control the traffic in and out of a network. These can protect against threats from the Internet, blocking harmful programs and also blocking others from looking at sensitive data. Most businesses have a firewall to protect them. Businesses also use antivirus software to protect against viruses.

## Computer viruses

Computer viruses are programs that "infect" computers and spread from one to another. They will interfere with the computer, sometimes allowing hackers to steal information or damaging the computer or its programs. They are often spread without the user realizing it in ways such as email attachments, instant messaging, or Internet downloads. It is important for users to protect themselves against computer viruses. Programs like AVG and Norton Antivirus can scan and protect computers against viruses and should be updated regularly. It is important for users not to download files unless they are certain the source is secure. Some viruses will send out emails to a user's address book with the virus, so even if something is from a trusted source, it still might not be safe. Users should keep up to date on the most recent viruses and remove any as soon as they can.

## Issues regarding privacy and online marketing

There are many issues surrounding privacy and online marketing. Marketers use cookies to collect information about people without their knowledge. Many people do not realize how much information marketers have on them, information that is then sold and shared with others. Everything that someone enters into a website or social media site could be saved, shared, and used. There is also a great deal of spam that is sent to people, including mass unsolicited emails that fill up email inboxes. Sometimes these are scams and do not represent real opportunities or offers. It can be hard to distinguish between ethical and unethical marketing practices and people need to protect themselves as best they can by being careful with what they share and reading the privacy policies of companies.

## Legal issues regarding intellectual property with use of technology

Intellectual property refers to intangible things people have created with their minds. This includes written copy, artwork, phrases, designs, symbols, logos, and more. Protection comes in many forms, including copyrights, patents, and trademarks. With technology in business, these items may become less secure. For instance, an art company may put protected art on their website and then others may copy that artwork. Some companies may use copyrighted material (purposely or inadvertently) on websites such as a song by a famous singer. The laws protecting their use cover a range based on the type of property and other details, but there have been many court cases over improper use of protected material online. It can be more difficult for a company to protect its material if it is being sent to the entire Internet because it is easy to copy others' materials. These court cases will continue to define the laws.

## Use of technology in production systems

Robotics are often utilized to piece together products or perform other production duties. They may move quicker or be more precise than humans. Computer-aided design lets people utilize computers when creating or modifying designs. They may use it to optimize a design or evaluate it. For instance, it may be used to create electronics. It can provide a great deal of information and views of the design. Computer-aided manufacturing is the use of computers to control the devices that manufacture workpieces. It seeks to accelerate the production process with improved material consistency and more accurate dimensions.

### Benefits and drawbacks
One benefit of utilizing technology with production systems is the cost savings. Companies may be able to save a lot of money in the long run by having computerized systems and lowering the need for paid employees. It can also make production more efficient and save time. The computerized system may be able to produce many more items at a quicker rate. It may also do a better job at making the items exactly as the company desires and exactly the same, helping with quality control. One drawback of a computerized production system is that there can be a high initial cost for the initial system. Although cost savings may be realized later, it can take a large output to get it set up. The system may allow for less flexibility than if people were doing it. Also, if there is a problem, it

can stop the entire line. Some companies are resistant to making change, and technology could result in job losses.

<u>Social and economic impact</u>
As companies use technology, they become more efficient and can save money, becoming more competitive. This can have a positive effect on an economy because the company will have an advantage over other companies and produce positive change. In some areas, however, this increased technology can mean a loss of jobs, which can be negative for the economy. When technology has allowed business to become more efficient, society can benefit. For instance, if it is less expensive to make products like cars, then more people can enjoy them. As technology improvements make production cheaper, more people will be able to enjoy these products.

**Educating employees in computers and technology**

Many businesses require employees to be educated in computers and technology. It is important to have efficient and effective procedures for doing so. First, employees should be evaluated for their current skills. Some employees may need little or no training, while others will need significant training. The students may be placed into groups based on abilities. Training sessions should be planned in advance so employees can learn before they are expected to perform the activities. Sometimes training will be on the job by another employee. Other times the business will get a computer program that will train the students or it might be done through live lectures or a video. Students should be evaluated after the training to ensure that it was effective. Training should be ongoing as necessary.

**Tailoring training to meet needs**

Technology training is not one size fits all. Businesses need to tailor the training to the needs of their business. For instance, training just a few employees is very different than training a large group of employees. A business that has just a few employees to train might have one employee train another. If a big group needs to be trained, however, then it may invest in customized computer training or videos that can handle a lot of people. Also, companies need to evaluate the employees before training because the training will very much depend on how skilled they already are. They may invest in computer training that can be tailored to the level the person is at. Companies should not waste time and resources training employees on knowledge they already have. These employees may be trained more in the specifics of the job than common computer knowledge.

**Evaluating employees on computer knowledge before and after training**

It is important for a company to ensure that its computer training program is effective by evaluating employees both before and after training. There are various methods to accomplish this. Many computer-based training programs come with a pre-training and post-training evaluation. The employee will take a test on the computer that will evaluate his or her computer competency. This might be in general computer use, in something specific to the job position, or both. Sometimes it is a simulation of the job the employee will be performing. After the training, the employee will receive the same or a similar test to ascertain whether the training was effective. This test could also be given on paper. Another way to evaluate an employee is to have the employee try to do computer functions in front of someone knowledgeable. The person can evaluate the employee on his (or her) computer skills before and after training.

## Developing and implementing technological support for employees

A company must determine its needs, which will largely be determined by the complexity of computer systems as well as the size of the company. Many larger companies have an information technology (IT) department, which is responsible for making sure the technology is running smoothly and provides a contact point for employees who are having difficulty. Some companies that are smaller may instead contract with another company that can provide IT support. Of course, one can sometimes contact the vendor of the computer product. Some very small companies may have employees who are not specifically assigned to IT, but who are computer literate and help with problems. Companies may also provide support on websites. They may provide a list of common complaints, for instance, or provide other information. Many companies combine various forms of IT support.

## Hardware and computer peripherals utilized in business

Memory storage devices allow users to store data. These come in many different sizes and connect in different ways. Some companies may get an external hard drive to provide more space. Flash drives make it easy to share information between people or carry files on the go. There are a number of devices used to connect to the Internet. Modems allow this. Routers create networks that pass and direct data. Scanners create digital copies from physical ones. For instance, companies can scan in receipts to cut back on paper and have a secure digital file. Printers are used to print documents. Other common peripherals include the keyboard, which is used to input data; the mouse, which allows people to select items; and the microphone and camera, which allow for video conferencing.

## Common computer operations utilized in business

One very useful computer operation is file management. Companies typically have a lot of files, and they need to be able to manage, sort, store, and access them efficiently. For instance, an insurance company will have a wide range of files for its different clients. There are many file management programs that allow companies to easily manage their files. Network operations involve the management and maintenance of a telecommunications network. Computers allow users to communicate with each other in various ways such as email. Companies also use computers for data backup. They can send information offsite so that even if something catastrophic happens to the first source of data, the data will remain secure in another location. There are also specific shutdown procedures that make everything easy and logical. It is important to close all programs and then use the Shut Down button located on the Start menu.

## Basic troubleshooting of computer problems

Not every computer problem requires a call to the IT department. Users can do some simple troubleshooting on their own first. They should write down everything they do, as well as any error messages they receive, in case the problem needs to be escalated. The first thing to do is make sure all the cables and cords are properly connected. They should make sure the outlet or surge protector has power and that the monitor and speakers are on. A simple closing and reopening of a program or restarting the computer in general is often enough to fix the problem. The company may have a source where they list updates and/or identified issues. If the computer or program is frozen, users should press Control/Alt/Delete (Option/Command/Esc on a Mac) to access the task manager where they can select and end the task that is giving them problems. A "non-system disk or disk error" message may mean the user needs to remove a CD, flash drive, DVD, or floppy disk

- 49 -

before booting up. If the user can't get it to shut down, he can hold down the power button to do it. He can also run antivirus software to scan for problems.

## Laptop computers

Laptops are used very often in business. They are produced from companies such as Dell, Toshiba, and Acer. They are very useful and allow a business professional to take all the features of his computer wherever he goes, including on business trips. Businessmen commonly use them for communication. They will email people and also use them for video conferencing. They can use them for word processing such as writing business letters. They can use them to create and show presentations to clients, customers, or business partners. They can use them to store business information. Especially for someone who travels a lot, this can be very important. Smartphones can also do a lot, but they cannot compare to a full computer. Laptops provide this convenience for many in the business world.

## PDAs

Personal digital assistants (PDAs) are like small computers, similar to smartphones without the phone capability. For the most part they have been replaced with smartphones. They provide a wealth of information and give the user connection to the Internet. They typically contain a calendar, schedule, listing of contact information, notes program, and calculator. They make it easy for businessmen to carry information with them (especially before smartphones became widely available) and to access the Internet and all the advantages it provides. They range greatly in features, brands, and price. Most also allow for a form of portable memory to carry information. Some people still use them.

## Smartphones

Smartphones are very commonly used in business. First, they allow people to make and receive phone calls while on the go, which is especially valuable for someone who is rarely at his (or her) desk. Businessmen can also contact others through a wide variety of functions such as texting, email, and Skype. They can conduct videoconferencing while on the go. Smartphones also allow businessmen to access the information of the Internet. They can show off their websites to clients, for instance. They can access social media where they can post things about the business. There are many apps that may be useful for businessmen. They can access the GPS while on a business trip, or check the weather when planning an outdoor event. They can use it to set reminders and alarms or manage their schedules. They can use it to carry presentations. There are many smartphones, including the popular iPhone series, and Android-based phones.

## Software often utilized in business

Word processing programs allow users to create, read, edit, and manipulate documents. Database management software allows companies to manage their databases. It both manages and analyzes data. There are a lot of specialized programs that allow users to forecast sales and get other data. Spreadsheet software allows users to make spreadsheets and tables and calculate information. Excel is a popular one. Companies also use presentation programs to create, edit, and view presentations. There are a number of software programs related to communication. These allow for email as well as video conferencing and other forms of communication. Many companies have specific programs for accounting and operations. These can help a company manage its business more effectively. Within each of these categories are a wide range of software choices.

## Word processing software

Word processing software allows users to create, read, edit, save, and format documents. These are often based in text, but may have images as well. They may have tables and other features. They are used very frequently in business for everything from business letters to resumes to company reports and more. The formatting options in the modern programs are vast and allow for great customization of the documents. They also allow a lot of shortcuts to make it quick and easy to create a document as well as tools to make a quality document such as a spelling and grammar checker. There are a number of word processing programs, and Microsoft Word (from Microsoft Office) is one of the most widely used. Other popular programs include WordPerfect (Corel Corporation), Writer (OpenOffice by Apache), and Pages (Apple Inc.).

## Database management software

Decision support systems are popular. These computerized information systems help managers make decisions. They are interactive and take data, business models, and other information such as sales data to calculate valuable information. They might compare sales numbers, project revenue, or project the consequences of different moves, for instance. A database management system (DBMS) is another system that lets users create, store, change, and view information from a database. They range greatly in size as well as technical specifications and may be organized in a relational, flat, network, or hierarchical manner, with relational being the most common. They preserve the data's integrity. Structured Query Language (SQL) is the standard interface.

## Spreadsheet software

Spreadsheet software allows users to create spreadsheets, making it easy to view information. These programs allow for calculations and manipulations of the data. For instance, a businessman can calculate payroll deductions or average sales results. Microsoft Excel is one of the most common spreadsheet software programs used today. It has columns (denoted by letters) and rows (denoted by numbers), and the current cell is called the Active Cell, which is denoted by the letter of the column and number of the row. It is useful to know the basic Excel formulas for calculations. First, a user starts with the equal sign and then the formula. For instance, if he wanted the D4 cell to be the sum of C1 and C2, then he would put in the formula =C1+C2. Users can also make a similar formula with subtraction (-), multiplication (*) and division (/). They can put more than one of these in a formula. Also, to add a range of values, users can use the SUM function. For instance, SUM(B1:B3) adds the values of B1, B2, and B3.

## Traditional software

With traditional, or closed-source software, the software owners do not allow others to see or modify their code. This is the case with many of the large programs like Microsoft Office. Companies may prefer it because they do not want anyone changing or stealing their code. Users might like knowing exactly what a program will contain when they get it and not worry about changes to the code. There are disadvantages for users, however. Users cannot go into the code to add or disable features. When the code is open-source, people can look through and fix bugs, but this is not possible with closed-source.

## Open-source software

Open-source software is software that has the source code available to people for viewing, modification, and enhancement. Individuals can go in to the source code and take out things they do not like or add code to create additional features. It is advantageous because people can make improvements or disable parts of the code they do not wish to utilize. People can also spot errors in the code. They can adapt it for their own needs and then pass it on, so others can take advantage of the new features and altered programming. It also helps teach individuals how to program and understand code. Many companies choose not to do open-source code because they do not wish others to change their programs.

## Techniques to input data on computers

There are many special function keys and shortcuts that allow users to perform myriad functions on the computer. The Tab key moves the cursor to the following tab stop. The Insert key changes the inputting between the overtype mode, in which it overtypes existing text; and insert mode, in which the existing characters are forced one forward to make room for the new character. The Home key moves the cursor to the start of the line or to the start of the document if the text cannot be edited. There are a number of key combinations that make it easy to perform tasks. Many of these use the Control (Ctrl) key, which is combined with another key to perform a function. Some of the popular ones are Copy (Ctrl and C), Undo (Ctrl and Z), Cut (Ctrl and X), Paste (Ctrl and V), Select all (Ctrl and A), New browser window (Ctrl and N), Terminate application or restart computer (Ctrl and Alt and Delete), Find (Ctrl and F), and Save document (Ctrl and S). Users can also access special features on the computer such as the spell checker through the Review tab, Proofing group, and Spelling & Grammar option.

## Find and Replace functions on computers

The Find and Replace functions allow a user to find one or more characters in a document and then (if the user chooses) replace it with a different characters or characters. The user can go through the document to view every time the characters appear, or just replace them all. To access it, users can either click on the Find icon (the word or binoculars) or press down Control (Ctrl) and the letter F. The user will then type in the characters to be searched for and can choose options such as matching case and whole words only. They can click on Find or Enter. They can then go to Replace (which might show up right away or be in its own tab, depending on the computer program) and type what is to replace the item. The user can specify whether to replace one or all of them at the same time.

## Techniques to format documents

There are many options to format a document in popular word processing programs such as Microsoft Word. A user can change the font style and size in the drop down box in the Home tab. He (or she) can go to the paragraph option to justify text, change line spacing and change indentation. He can click the appropriate icon to create a numbered or bulleted list. The page layout page has a number of options. In the page setup section, a person can click on the columns tab to make columns. He can change the margins and orientation from the tabs of the same name. In the page background section, he can add a watermark or change page colors or page borders. When he clicks on the icon, he will be taken to an easy-to-understand menu that provides options such as type and thickness of border. The Insert tab allows users to insert a variety of elements such as tables, pictures, and clip art. They can insert a page break, blank page, or cover page in the pages section. There is also a header and footer section where these can be inserted and formatted.

## Making, formatting, and modifying tables on computers

It is simple to make, format, and modify a table on the computer. Users should go to the Insert tab and click on the Table icon, where they can specify the size of the table. It has some built-in templates for tables such as a calendar, a matrix, and a tabular list. Users can also draw a table to customize it to their exact specifications by using the Draw Table option. Once the table is created, the user can go to the table tools design tab to specify things like banded rows, banded columns, table style, shading, and borders. Users can type in the tables. They can go to the layout section under table tools to make further formatting changes such as changing cell margins and text direction, managing properties of tables, inserting rows and columns, specifying height and width, and more. It is very flexible and allows users to modify the text and format to whatever they want.

## Common toolbar icons

There are a number of common icons seen in the toolbar. A small printer means print. An arrow pointing left means to go back, while one pointing right means to go forward. A house in a browser means to go to the home page. Arrows by the address bar mean refresh, while an X means stop. Sometimes refresh is a circle with an arrow. A star may save it to favorites. In Word, a page icon makes a new blank document. Clicking on the floppy disk will save it. Scissors will cut the selection, two pages with writing next to it will copy it, and a clipboard will paste it. A curved left arrow will undo the last step, while a curved right arrow will redo it. An open file icon will open a file. A checkmark with ABC will open the spelling, grammar, and writing style checker. The icon with two columns of lines will change the amount of columns while the little table icon will create a table. These icons range depending on the program and computer system.

# Law and International Business

## Benefits of international trade

There are many benefits to international trade. One advantage is that a company has an entirely new market to which to sell. It can increase its sales and thus its profits tremendously by reaching these customers. A company may have surplus supply that would otherwise not be utilized. Customers can enjoy products that are not available domestically. If international trade was not available, they may not be able to get that product. Also, opening up international trade can make those products available for less money. They may get the foreign product for cheaper, and even domestic companies may lower the prices to become more competitive. Consumers who wouldn't have been able to afford the products may now do so. Also, there is less dependence on a single market, so if something goes wrong, the item will still be available. A foreign market may be more profitable for a domestic company.

## Drawbacks of international trade

There are a lot of arguments against free trade. It can lead to job losses and company failures domestically. New domestic companies may not have a chance to catch up with foreign companies. Some feel that it is risky, especially if getting products from rival countries. Also, there are concerns about working conditions. In some countries, there is little regulation and people work in unsafe and unsanitary conditions. Workers, including children, may work many hours for little pay. Also, the manufacturing processes may damage the environment. There might not be the same quality control for the products, and some of the products may be of lower quality or even hazardous. Also, when jobs are outsourced, there will be less opportunity in the United States. Domestic companies that have good practices and fairly compensated employees may have difficulty competing with international companies that do not. A company may also face barriers to trade such as quotas, tariffs, and cultural resistance.

## Historical patterns of international trade

The United States has engaged in international trade for many centuries. The triangular trade system was a system that ran from the late 1500s to the early 1800s. It connected Africa, the American colonies, and the Caribbean and consisted of slaves, crops, and manufactured goods. Many countries export raw goods and import manufactured materials. The United States trades with a wide variety of countries, and many companies have gone international through trade. The country has practiced protectionism, but has gravitated towards free trade in modern days. Still, protectionism is not eradicated and can be seen in policies today.

## Modern trends in international business

There have been many trends in international business. Much of the manufacturing has moved internationally to areas where the cost of labor is lower. China has emerged as a significant exporter, with many of the goods in the United States and other countries coming from there. Multinational businesses have a great impact on the growth and health of the economy, especially given their size. They add a lot to the growth of the GDP. Trade also plays a large part in economic growth, both in the United States and other countries. There have also been some trends in the United States. The country has increased the importation of oil. Approximately half of the oil import originates from the Western Hemisphere. Also, the United States currently has a negative balance of trade, also known as a trade deficit. This means the United States is importing more than it is exporting.

## Economic factors that influence international trade

There are various economic factors that influence international trade. One is opportunity costs. Opportunity costs are what a producer gives up by choosing a different option. For instance, if a producer can make a dozen cookies in an hour or a dozen brownies in an hour for the same cost and he chooses to make the cookies, then the dozen brownies are the opportunity cost. Someone who has a higher opportunity cost for making a product may want to import that product so they do not have to incur the opportunity cost. Comparative advantage is given to the party with the lowest opportunity cost. It makes sense for them to produce and export it. Absolute advantage is when a producer can make more of something with smaller inputs. For instance, if one country can make 10 shirts for the cost and effort that another country uses to make five shirts, then the country that can make more has the absolute advantage. It makes sense for the producer who can make it with the least inputs to make it.

## Government policies that create an obstacle to international trade

There are many government policies that create an obstacle to international trade. These are done for different reasons, including protecting domestic businesses and raising revenues. Quotas put a restriction on the amount of imports. Beyond that number, the products must be made by domestic means. This can make products more expensive because it may be more expensive to make domestically, although domestic companies gain because they can charge more. The government also wins with more tax revenues. Tariffs are taxes that apply to goods that are imported. Because the cost of imports is increased, domestic production is cheaper. This is advantageous for domestic manufacturers. Voluntary export restraints are self-applied rules that restrict what a country can export to another country. Oftentimes the importing country has requested the limit. Embargoes occur when a country restricts trade with a specific foreign country. It is often for political or economic reasons. These measures are often done concurrently.

## Effects of currency exchange rates on trade

When a country purchases items from another country, they first change their money over to that currency. When the foreign currency is weaker, they can purchase more of it for their own money. They will then have more money and the items will be relatively cheaper. They will import more from the country with the weaker currency because these items are less expensive. Alternatively, if a country is trading with a country that has a stronger form of currency, then they will be able to get less of that foreign money and thus the goods will be more expensive. They might import less in this case. Exchange rates change constantly, thus so does trade.

## Benefits and drawbacks of a weak/strong dollar

Whether the dollar is weak or strong can make a big difference for the economy and everyday people. If the dollar is weak, it has less purchasing power and it becomes more expensive to import from foreign countries. As prices increase, consumers spend less. Fuel costs tend to go up, too. Inflation can occur because of this. Central banks might raise interest rates to attract investors, but this can be problematic for the economy. A benefit of a weak dollar is that a trade deficit could decrease and domestic job growth can occur, especially in industries like manufacturing. Demand will also increase for exports because they are cheaper, which will also increase jobs. There could be some lost jobs, however, from businesses that are paying more for supplies. A strong dollar makes the opposite occur. Foreign goods cost less, so importing may increase while exporting or domestically-produced items go down. Prices can go down as well. One is not necessarily bad or good. Overall, a strong economy will have a strong dollar, but sometimes a weak dollar is best.

## Elements that influence international trade

Balances of trade, the differential between a nation's imports and exports, can influence international trade. So can the balance of payments, which is a compilation of economic transactions of a nation and the global companies with which it trades. It includes loan repayment, capital movements, money spent by tourists, and more. International trade is also affected by changes in the supply of labor as well as demand for labor. If a lower supply of labor exists, a country may need to import more and vice versa. Some countries also have practices such as dumping. This is where a country exports products at an extremely low price compared to what they would be available for domestically. This can be catastrophic for manufacturers in that country. Sometimes countries will also take retaliatory actions that can affect international trade. The exchange rates and values of the different currencies also matter. If a country's currency is strong, it has more power and might import more; if it is weak, it might import less. All of these factors combine to affect international trade.

## GATT

The General Agreement on Tariffs and Trade (GATT) is a treaty that was formed after World War II to help the economy. It strives to lower obstacles to global trade such as quotas, tariffs, and subsidies. It played a huge part in increasing free trade throughout the 20th century. The main part was for trade to occur without discrimination. A country had its markets opened equally to other countries. If a country made an agreement to lower tariffs with the countries it had a significant trade with, then those went to other GATT members, too. The nations would specify the tariff rates they would provide to the other member countries. GATT also strove to promote tariffs rather than a limit on the number of items traded. There was an escape clause in case a country lost a lot because of concessions in trade. It was in effect until the World Trade Organization took over in 1995, at which point it had 125 nations signed to it and governed 90 percent of international trade.

## NAFTA

The North American Free Trade Agreement (NAFTA) became active in 1994 and has had a profound effect on trade ever since. The agreement was signed by the United States, Mexico, and Canada and, as part of it, number restrictions and duties were terminated on January 1, 2008. The largest international free trade area was formed, and trade between the three countries increased tremendously, going to 1.2 trillion for US goods and services in 2012. Canada benefited economically from the agreement. Mexico has a lot of factories known as maquiladoras that take raw goods and make them into finished products. The United Sates has seen trade increase tremendously, but there has been loss of manufacturing jobs to Mexico. There were some issues about environmental concerns, thus the North American Agreement on Environmental Cooperation (NAAEC) was formed to address this. There were some increases in pollution. There have been many benefits overall.

## WTO

Started in 1995 by the Marrakech Agreement, the World Trade Organization (WTO) is an international organization related to trade rules between different countries. WTO agreements are negotiated and created to form agreements that benefit producers, importers and exporters. It provides a place for companies to negotiate trade and work through problems such as problems restricting trade. It has formed trade rules. It works to promote safe and effective trade without conflicts between nations. It helps nations come up with their own trade agreements. It also helps resolve disputes and ensure nations comply with agreements they have made. It has a staff of more than 600 people in Geneva, Switzerland.

## IMF

Part of the United Nations, the International Monetary Fund (IMF) promotes economic stability in 188 member countries. It strives for international growth by giving advice in policies. It also helps developing nations reduce the level of poverty. It works to keep exchange rates stable and international trade balanced. It provides financing to countries having difficulty and gives training and technical assistance. It also works with research and tries to keep the international financial system stable. It performs surveillance to keep track of economic or financial problems. It will appraise the situations and help countries create policies that are best. It also looks at economic trends worldwide. There is some criticism of the organization based on several issues, like reports that the loan conditions are too intrusive and intervene too much by forcing privatization, for instance. Critics also argue the policies of the Washington consensus are put forth without considering the special needs of that country, that policies are expected to be implemented together right away, and that the organization doesn't take criticism well.

## World Bank

The World Bank works to reduce poverty by loaning money to developing countries for capital programs. This international financial organization is part of the United Nations. It promotes foreign investment, international trade, and capital investment. It also works to improve health and fight diseases such as AIDS, tuberculosis, and malaria by sending vaccines internationally and other measures. It has also fought for environmental causes such as preventing climate change. It is now focused on 14 centralized global practices, including health and water. There has been some criticism, with some based on upcoming layoffs and lowered budgets. It is based in Washington, D.C.

## Conducting international business through licensing

International business is often conducted through licensing. International licensing occurs when one business makes an agreement with another, giving special permission to make the product in a foreign country. It might involve the resources to do it or the right. This might include a copyright, skills of managers, patents, technology, and more. It is advantageous in that companies can get into new markets they may not have been able to enter through other means because of restrictions in trade. It is also a way to enter another market without spending too much money or incurring too much risk because the company is just giving the rights and resources to make the product and not actually going in and doing it itself. The disadvantage is that there is a risk that the foreign firm will not adhere to the agreement. Also, with lower financial involvement and risk comes a lower expected financial return.

## Conducting international business through franchising

One way to conduct international business is through franchising. This is where an individual leases the ability to replicate a business model and brand. Generally, the individual will create a business that is a replica of a successful one. For instance, a franchise restaurant will have the same look, food, etc. McDonald's is a common franchise. There are both advantages and disadvantages to conducting international business through franchising. The model has already been successful and people are accustomed to it, so it may already have a built-in audience, which can stimulate business from the beginning. Domestic success may not translate to international success, however. Tastes and preferences are different in other countries. One advantage is that much of the work is done—the person will already have the branding, the products, and so forth created. The franchisee may be subject to laws and regulations in other countries, however. Also, the franchisee may have little control and be unable to change things. Entrepreneurs should consider all these factors when deciding whether to franchise.

## Conducting international business through contract manufacturing

Contract manufacturing is a popular method of entering a foreign market. With contract manufacturing, the company designs the product but then hires another company to manufacture and ship it. This can be a very cost effective way of doing business, especially in foreign markets where it might be more expensive to do business. Also, companies can find a manufacturer that is able to make a product that they do not have the ability to make. It will also free the company to focus on designing the products and other things. There are risks as well. The company will not have as much control over the product and it may not come out with the desired quality. Also, some foreign companies have poor practices with regard to working conditions or the environment. The company will also be sharing their intellectual property, which they risk losing. If there is a problem, it will reflect on the company. Also, sometimes there are contract disputes or other issues with the relationship. Overall, contract manufacturing can be a great way to enter a foreign business as long as the risks are considered.

## Conducting international business through joint ventures

One common method for conducting international business is through joint ventures. In this strategy, a company will form a partnership with a company in the international market it wants to enter. Both inputs and outputs, such as profits or losses, are shared. It can be short or long term, but is often temporary. It is advantageous in that the risk is shared. It is less risky to a business entering the foreign market. In addition, the business can take advantage of the fact that the foreign business is already familiar with the market in the other country. Also, consumers may be less resistant to them because they will seem to be part of the local business and not a foreign entity. Sometimes there are laws and regulations that would make it difficult for a foreign business to enter the market otherwise. The downside is the company will share the profits from the venture. Also, the company may have to give up some decision-making power. Sometimes disagreements arise from partnerships. With proper research it can be an excellent way to enter an international market.

## Conducting international business through strategic alliances

A common method of conducting international business is through strategic alliances. It is similar to a joint venture in that two companies—one domestic and one foreign—come to an agreement to work on a project to benefit both of them. They may share resources. Whereas in a joint venture the company may form an actual business entity together, with a strategic alliance they work together on a project, but the firms remain independent. Also, it is typically not as long or involved as a joint venture. It is advantageous because a company can get into a foreign market it may otherwise have difficulty entering. It can use the benefits of the foreign company's knowledge and reputation in that country and help avoid resistance to a foreign business. The businesses can also share the risk. Of course, the company will not have full control over the project and may be responsible if the other company does something wrong. They will also have to share the rewards such as profit.

## Conducting international business through foreign subsidiaries

When a company opens a new subsidiary in a foreign country, either by starting one or buying an existing company, it is called a foreign subsidiary. The advantage is that the parent company stays in charge of the subsidiary and makes the decisions. They can get the rewards of it, and also enjoy cost savings when the parent and subsidiary share the same resources such as the same financial processes. A disadvantage is that they can be liable for the subsidiary's problems. If the parent company starts a business from the beginning, it will have to deal with the difficulties of establishing a business in a foreign country such as finding customers and suppliers. Buying an established business can ease some of these difficulties. It can be very expensive to get into international business this way, and it is a large commitment. Still, it can expand a business' customers, sales, and profit.

## Factors to consider when entering international business

There are many factors that businesses should consider when entering international business. First, they should think about how their product is likely to do overseas. Consumers have different tastes and preferences in different areas; the company should make sure there is a demand for their product. They should conduct market research. Sometimes a product can be successful but only with changes to the product, branding, pricing, or marketing. They should also consider the competition. Businesses should look at the laws, regulations, and licensing requirements, which may be very different from those in the United States. The company should consider the logistics and costs of expanding internationally. It may cost a lot more to ship products overseas. The company needs to consider exactly how it will penetrate the international market. There are many methods for international penetration; the company should research these to find out what is best for them. They may want to research alliances with others in the foreign area. They should make a clear business plan for penetrating the market.

## Influences of cultural, economic, sociopolitical, and language differences on international business

Laws and regulations can be different in different countries, including those pertaining to business. Businessmen need to be sure to understand the laws in the country in which they are doing business. The culture can have a significant effect. Some cultures are much more formal than others. Certain practices, such as touching someone, are taboo in certain cultures. Businessmen need to know what is acceptable. Also, there can be language barriers and someone may accidently convey the wrong meaning. It is important to have someone who knows the language well and can translate successfully. There can also be political issues as well. Some countries are more restrictive on what can be advertised and how. They may have restrictions. Businesses should understand how distribution channels work. When a business plans to enter a foreign market, they should do research to make sure they understand the cultural, economic, sociopolitical, and language factors at play.

## Ethnocentrism and stereotyping

Cultures across the globe are very different, and it can be difficult to communicate between these lines. This has led to some mistaken beliefs and practices. Ethnocentrism occurs when a people believe that they and their culture are superior to those of others. It is extremely common and can affect international business greatly. People of one culture may be very resistant to businesses from other countries because they feel they are not as good. Stereotyping can occur in which people believe certain things about a people just because of who they are. They may believe everyone from a certain country is bad, for instance. When consumers are ethnocentric and have stereotypes, they may reject products from international companies and prefer those from their country. Certain countries display these characteristics more than others. This can affect international business greatly.

## Criminal and civil law

Criminal law involves someone accused of a crime. The individual broke a law and did something detrimental to society. Although it might involve a victim, that victim does not have to be the one to bring the case to life; the government (in the form of prosecution) will. There doesn't have to be a victim such as if someone was caught driving under the influence but did not hurt anyone. If the person is found guilty, he may have to pay money, could be sentenced to prison, and (in rare cases) executed. A civil case is a dispute between two parties. They are brought by one party against another because of a failure of a legal duty. The plaintiff may ask for compensation or for the party to fulfill the duty, but the defendant cannot be sentenced to prison or death. They both can occur in local or federal courts. Lawyers can be used for both, but are guaranteed for criminal defendants. Because of the seriousness of criminal law, defendants are presumed innocent and the state must prove the charges beyond a reasonable doubt. It is less difficult in civil cases.

## Case, administrative, statutory, constitutional, and tort law

Criminal law deals with crimes that are committed. Case law refers to the verdicts of courts that can now be used in new court cases to help plead cases and define the law. Statutory law refers to codes and statutes the legislative bodies have enacted. Administrative law refers to the procedures that administrative agencies create. It is very technical. Different agencies have different procedures and these must be fulfilled before a lawsuit can be brought. Constitutional law refers to how the United States Constitution is interpreted and implemented. Tort law refers to civil claims that one party brings against another. A plaintiff claims that a defendant harmed him in a way that constitutes a legal liability. Some attorneys specialize in one type of law while others practice a broader range.

## Lawsuits

A lawsuit occurs when one party brings a case against another party in a court of law. It is also known as a civil action. The plaintiff makes the complaint that the other party (defendant) did something for which they are legally liable. Unlike criminal cases, a person's freedom is not in jeopardy—there is no prison sentence. The person may not have broken a law to have a lawsuit brought against him (or her). It can also involve negligence. The person may ask for compensatory damages, which compensate the plaintiff for the money he may have lost, as well as pain and suffering. There might also be punitive damages, which is like a punishment for being malicious, reckless, or grossly negligent. One person files the suit, followed by discovery, any pre-trial motions, and oftentimes discussions of settlement. If it doesn't get settled, then it will go to a trial and the judgment. Finally, one party can appeal. Sometimes, parties will come together to make a lawsuit as a group, which can appear much stronger because of the amount of people. This is called a class action lawsuit.

## Court systems

There are many different court systems in the United States, including a federal court system and state courts. State court systems consist of many different tiers. State trial courts may consist of county courts, circuit courts, and city or municipal courts, among others. Trial courts may have limited jurisdiction, hearing lower criminal charges, cases involving juveniles, traffic issues, and some civil cases. More serious cases, such as those with more serious crimes or higher stakes civil cases, may go to a court of general jurisdiction. These may include circuit courts, superior courts, or courts of common pleas. There are specialized courts in many states. These include courts such as family courts and juvenile courts. States usually also have a supreme court where cases that have worked their way up the lower courts can be heard. Federal courts are generally divided into circuits and districts, with at least one per state. Many federal lawsuits are heard in those. The highest court is the US Supreme Court, which shapes many laws. It hears a small number of very important cases.

## Due process, liability, damages, burden of proof, and negligence

Due process refers to a person's right to have the state respect his legal rights. It is about providing fairness to those involved in legal matters such as by providing a notice of rights. Liability refers to a party's legal responsibility for behaviors, actions, or inactions. If someone does not meet his (or her) duty, he could have a lawsuit brought against him. Damages refer to the money that may be given to the plaintiff from the defendant during a lawsuit. The plaintiff with a civil lawsuit has the responsibility of providing burden of proof, which means he must bring a "preponderance of evidence" or "weight of evidence" to show that he has enough facts to win the case. In criminal cases, burden of proof refers to a prosecutor needing to show that the defendant is guilty "beyond a reasonable doubt." Negligence is when a party does not show a reasonable amount of care. Though accidental, a reasonable person would have acted differently. One can be liable for this.

## Laws and regulations that affect business

There are a wide variety of laws and regulations that affect business. Business or corporate law refers to the laws surrounding how corporations are formed, dissolved, and run. Labor laws deal with many aspects of the relationship between employer and employee such as working conditions, wages, and discrimination. Tax law deals with the taxes that businesses owe. Contract laws govern the contracts that many businesses enter into on a regular basis. Property law governs how property is owned, commonly seen in business. Antitrust law strives to keep a competitive marketplace by not allowing mergers that would form monopolies and other antitrust activities. The Uniform Commercial Code (UCC) helps make transactions easier between states by helping make uniformity in commercial laws. Companies are also subject to accounting and financial management laws, as well as laws regarding their insurance and credit.

## FTC

Formed in 1914, the Federal Trade Commission (FTC) protects consumers by stopping businesses from performing deceptive, unfair, and anticompetitive practices. It strives to stop fraud and other types of deception and keep competition fair by stopping anticompetitive mergers. It is a federal agency that has competition jurisdiction and consumer protection jurisdiction. It helps make policies and shares information with the legislature and government agencies. When wrongdoing is suspected, the FTC will investigate and, at times, sue to stop it. They accept complaints about businesses regarding many matters including identity theft, deceptive advertising, and data security. They pass the information along to law enforcement agencies when appropriate. They also work to prevent mergers that would create anticompetitive organizations such as monopolies. They have had a large impact on the marketplace.

## SEC

The United States Securities and Exchange Commission (SEC) plays a large role in protecting investors, maintaining the integrity of the market, and aiding in the formatting of capital. It works to keep a fair market without unfair practices that would be detrimental to investors. It makes, investigates, and enforces requirements of fair disclosure of information so that one party does not have insider information that would compromise the market's fairness. Companies are required to disclose information on a regular basis so that investors can make informed decisions. It also investigates evidence of fraud. If the SEC finds a violation such as insider trading, a company purposely providing false information, or accounting fraud, it will bring a civil enforcement action against the party. It is led by five commissioners who are appointed by the president. Its main functions include making sure that federal securities laws are enforced; making rules; making sure brokers, securities firms, ratings agencies and investment advisors are inspected; watching private regulatory organizations; and working with authorities to coordinate United States securities regulations.

## Sarbanes-Oxley Act and Bankruptcy Reform Act of 2005

Two acts that played a large part in business were the Sarbanes-Oxley Act and Bankruptcy Reform Act of 2005. The Sarbanes-Oxley Act was signed by President George W. Bush in 2002 and increased corporate responsibility and financial disclosure while fighting accounting and corporate fraud. It included new or improved standards for management firms, public accounting firms, and United States public company boards. It also led to the creation of the Public Company Accounting Oversight Board (PCAOB), which oversees auditing professionals. It was created in an effort to prevent corporate scandals at a time when such scandals were becoming common. It also made some types of misconduct crimes. The Bankruptcy Reform Act of 2005 was created to lower Bankruptcy Code filings. Parties filing for bankruptcy would now need to get financial counseling first. In addition, they would have to undergo a "means test" to see if they qualified. Filers had to wait eight years before using Chapter 7 bankruptcy again. In addition, it created a limit of $125,000 for homestead exemptions if the property was acquired within three years and a weakened automatic stay for multiple filers. This made it more difficult for people to file for Chapter 7 bankruptcy.

## Consumer protection laws

There are a number of consumer protection laws that safeguard individuals from unscrupulous business practices. Many of these laws are related to food safety and sanitation. Food must be handled, stored, and prepared in certain ways to prevent health hazards. For instance, meat must be stored at certain temperatures and can only stay out for a certain amount of time. The Food and Drug Administration (FDA), Department of Agriculture (USDA) and Food Safety and Inspection Service (FSIS) all play a part in administering these laws. There are also laws about credit and warranties. For instance, the Federal Warranty Law covers written and implied warranties. There are a number of laws about credit that the Federal Trade Commission enforces such as the Truth in

Lending Act (TILA), Fair Credit Reporting Act (FCRA), and Fair Debt Collection Practices Act (FDCPA). Additionally, unfair trade practices, such as misrepresentation and fraud, are banned. Many states have enacted laws against these, and consumers can complain to the appropriate consumer protection agency.

## Agencies related to consumer protection

The Federal Trade Commission is a national agency that protects consumers by taking complaints about unfair practices and stopping forbidden acts such as anticompetitive mergers. There are a wide variety of state, regional, and local agencies that provide the same services on a more local basis. These are often in the attorney general's office. They accept complaints, investigate claims, and take action as necessary. Another agency that provides consumer services is the Better Business Bureau (BBB). The BBB keeps records on companies and list complaints. When people make a complaint, the BBB will contact the company and try to get it resolved. Businesses that have a good record with the BBB can use it to their advantage. Many consumers look up companies on the BBB website before doing business, thus many companies strive to keep good records. Sometimes consumers have a choice of several agencies from which to choose when making complaints.

## Product testing and safety

### Laws
The Consumer Product Safety Act (1972) and the subsequent Consumer Product Safety Improvement Act address safety in toys, chemicals in products, and more. The government tests products, makes safety standards, and bans products it deems unsafe. There are numerous product labeling laws as well. The Fair Packaging and Labeling Act (FPLA) requires commodity producers to label the name of the product, the identity and source of the manufacturer, the distributor or packer, and the net quantity. It strives to help consumers understand what they are getting. There are laws that specifically regard food standards, like federal grading of meat products. As a result of the Federal Food, Drug, and Cosmetic Act, the US Food and Drug Administration (FDA) requires testing on drugs to ensure their safety and efficacy. They also monitor food and food additives for safety. Many agencies and laws help ensure product safety.

### Federal agencies
Part of the US Department of Health and Human Services, the Food and Drug Administration plays a large part in protecting consumers by overseeing the safety of food, drugs, and medical devices. They require extensive testing on drugs to ensure both efficacy and safety. They regulate food and labeling and give guidelines for the conditions in which food is prepared. They inform the public on related issues. The US Department of Agriculture (USDA) creates and executes policies in the fields of agriculture, farming, food, and forestry. They help rural communities, assist with conservation efforts, make rules regarding food and nutrition, make rules and standards for products labeled organic, and play many other roles. They have had a large impact throughout the years.

## Government agencies and laws concerning environmental protection

The Environmental Protection Agency (EPA) strives to safeguard the environment. Its roles include reducing the environmental impact of business practices; providing information; creating regulations and national standards based on laws from Congress; giving grants to non-profit organizations, state environmental programs, and schools; and performing research into environmental concerns. The EPA was formed in 1970, and its main headquarters is in Washington,

D.C. It has many programs based on specific issues such as fuel economy, air quality, and oil pollution, among others. There are a wide variety of laws to protect the environment in the United States such as the Clean Air Act, Clean Water Act, and Endangered Species Act. The EPA administers these and many more. Many of these also relate to business. The laws in other countries vary greatly, and many countries do not have the same environmental protections. Many international business agreements address these concerns.

## Ethical issues

### Conflicts of interest

A conflict of interest occurs when a person has two adversary interests, one of which might not be best for his (or her) business. An example is an employee of a general contractor who is making a decision on which of five bidding subcontractors to choose. If one of the subcontractors is his brother, he will have a conflict of interest because he might want to choose his brother, who might not be the best choice. He might choose his brother over someone better qualified. There are many instances of conflicts of interest in business. Oftentimes they are related to money. A person may accept gifts in exchange for a contract, for example. It is unethical to do something bad for the company because of personal interests. The employee should try to avoid this if possible. For instance, the person who works for the general contractor may ask someone else to make the decision so he doesn't have to choose between his brother and the company.

### Privacy of employees

There are a variety of ethical issues regarding the privacy of employees. Some of it stems from the monitoring of communications. Businesses can monitor employees' business calls, such as when a customer service agent is providing service to a customer, but it is murkier if employees are on personal calls. If employees are not supposed to be making personal calls at work, then employees may have the right to listen. Some people feel that it is not ethical, but then it is not ethical for employees to spend time on personal matters when they should be working. Most companies monitor Internet usage. Again, some people may worry about the ethical issues with privacy, but if it is on company time with company resources, the business could be liable for the employee's actions. A lot of companies perform background checks and drug testing, and this is allowed, although there are guidelines in place that must be followed. They must be reasonable. Most companies fulfill ethical duties by getting consent before performing the checks. It is very important for employers to keep records about the employees confidential.

### Compensation

Wages should be fair. It is important that one employee not make more or less for the wrong reasons. For instance, it is ethical for a company to pay more to an employee with more experience, but it is not ethical to pay more to a man than a woman solely because of gender. Still, this often happens, as does pay disparity among races, religions, and other categories. Sometimes advocates call out companies in which the top people make an exorbitant amount of money and the lower employees do very poorly. Ethical issues arise when people do not make a living wage. It is important to ensure pay disparity among workers is not occurring for the wrong reasons.

### Insider trading

Illegal insider trading occurs when someone makes a trade while having "insider" information that makes it unfair to other investors. This can occur when a corporate officer discovers something significant about a company and makes a trade because of that information. For instance, an employee may learn of a big problem about to occur and get rid of the stock before the price plummets. Insider trading can also be committed by employee friends, family, and acquaintances;

government employees; law or banking employees who deal with a company; or just anyone who manages to obtain the illegal information. It is unethical because it makes it unfair to investors who have to trade without this information. Insider trading is taken very seriously by the US Securities and Exchange Commission and has serious consequences.

## Business' social responsibility

Businesses have a social responsibility to their customers, employees, investors, and society in general. To their employees they should have fair labor practices. Employees should be treated fairly and without discrimination. Those companies that deal with international business have a responsibility to make sure laborers involved in their business are also treated fairly. They also have a responsibility to investors to try to build their money (in socially acceptable ways). To customers they should be fair, putting out quality products without deception. Business practices and tactics should be fair and not deceptive—they should not badmouth a competitor, for instance. There are different ways to be socially responsible to society as a whole. Businesses should have practices that do not harm the environment or animals or create unsafe waste. Many companies also give to charity. Some use fair trade products or sustainably grown and processed products. When companies show socially responsible practices, people take notice and may give them more business. Corporate social responsibility is the business' responsibility to both make money and act in a socially responsible way. This can include economic responsibility, legal responsibility, ethical responsibility and philanthropic responsibility.

# Marketing and Management

## Four Ps of marketing

### Product
The product itself is a very important part of marketing. This can be a physical good or an intangible service. The company needs to pay attention to the quality of the product to ensure it meets customer needs. They should consider its design; physical features (if it is a good) such as color, shape and texture; and the packaging it is in. For both goods and services, customer service needs to be considered before, during, and after the sale. How it is styled matters. If it is a service, the exact service and how it will be carried out should be considered. All of these factors should please the consumer.

### Price
Pricing is a very important decision for a product because it can impact sales and opinions on the product. There are many factors that go into pricing decisions. This includes the costs, including fixed, variable, and direct and indirect costs. It also includes the competition. If the market is saturated, the company may have to lower the product's price to compete. It also depends on the group they are targeting and how much they would be willing to pay. Some companies also price as part of a positioning strategy. Penetration pricing is when companies offer the product at a low price initially to increase sales and market share. Skimming is when a company instead has a high price and then lowers it to make it available to more and more of the market. With competition pricing, a company looks at competitors when pricing. In bundle pricing, they tie the product to other products. Cost-based pricing is done based on costs and the desired profit. With premium pricing, they price it high to show that it is exclusive. Companies use a variety of pricing practices depending on the product.

### Placement
The placement element of the four Ps of marketing refers to the distribution or how the product gets from the company to the consumer. It focuses on the distribution channels utilized as well as the elements involved such as order processing, inventory management, warehousing, and transportation. The goal is to make an efficient and effective distribution system that is as cost-effective as possible. It also includes where the storefront or business is located. Of course, many companies utilize the Internet to sell their goods and services and then ship the items to them. It has to be convenient to the customer.

### Promotion
No matter how great a product is, it will not do well if no one knows about it. This is why promotion is so important. Promotion is the act of marketing a product so that people become aware of it and hopefully want to purchase it. This can include many facets. One is public relations, including press releases, sponsorships, trade fairs and other unpaid promotions, and advertising and sales promotions. There are also different promotional strategies. In push marketing, businesses bring their products to customers such as a saleswoman spraying a perfume fragrance in a department store. New products can benefit from this. In pull marketing, businesses try to convince consumers to come to them through sales promotions, brand loyalty, and advertising dollars. Both are commonly used.

## Advertising

There are many forms of advertising, including print, television, online, and radio. Within each of these are subsets. For instance, online advertising includes banner and pop-up ads. Many companies use an assortment of different advertising techniques, some of which can support each other. The goals of advertising include reaching consumers, teaching consumers about a business' products, convincing people to purchase the product, building brand loyalty, increasing sales, and more. Typically marketers build advertising campaigns with a step-by-step process. First, they perform research to find out how best to advertise the product and their target market. Then, they create a budget. Next, they create the advertisements, often using a specific theme or idea. They decide on the type of media to be used and schedule it in the best way. Finally, they set the campaign in motion.

## Marketing research

Companies perform market research to learn about their customers and the factors that affect their company. It can go a long way to producing quality marketing campaigns. There are different types of marketing research. Sales research involves looking at the sales numbers and the strategies the company was taking when sales were high as well as when they were low. They could look at the times they did not do anything, and see how sales were then. The goal is to recreate the wins and avoid the losses. Companies also do product research. In this research, companies try to identify the characteristics of a product or service that will fulfill the customers' needs. It is done to help produce the best product that will satisfy the customer. Companies will also look at what products can be developed with existing and upcoming technology. Advertising research aims to make advertising more effective. For instance, a company may show an ad to a sample audience before releasing it widely to test its efficacy.

## MIS

A marketing information system (MIS) helps marketers make good decisions. It collects and analyzes internal and external data and then sends out that information so marketers can better make decisions. It includes user interfaces, which allow the marketers to evaluate and understand the data; application software; marketing databases; and system support. There are many software programs that create an MIS. It helps the company make decisions based on actual information and data. Business managers use it to better understand their customers and the right decisions to make. It can help them understand the marketing environment and its changes. A business manager might use it to come up with the right marketing plan.

## Collecting market data

Marketers collect as much market data as possible to help make marketing and business decisions. Marketing research can take many forms. Companies may give out surveys to ask consumers about their behavior. These can be done in person, by mail, by phone, online, or through email. They form focus groups to find out information. A group will come together to talk about and evaluate a product. They will also look at public records. The data may be primary data or secondary data. Primary research is when marketers do original research. For instance, they give out a new survey. With secondary data, marketers look for data that already exists. They may do an evaluation of several studies, for instance. Primary data can be specifically tailored to the company, but can be expensive. The company may not have the means or resources to collect it. It can be used to find the most up-to-date information, however. Secondary data can be much cheaper. Sometimes it is hard to find because companies don't always share their information. The data may be outdated or not exactly what the company needs.

## Marketing plans

A marketing plan is vital for any business. It gives a direction for marketing efforts, incorporates important research, and serves as a guide for the marketing team. It contains various information, including details on the target market, the company's competitive position, the various methods that will be used to reach the market, and strategies for differentiation. First, the marketing team should research the target market and the best ways in which to reach them. A marketing plan typically encompasses many tactics because different consumers can be reached different ways. Marketing activities may include print, television, and radio advertisements; sponsorships; press releases; a website; a social media presence; and more. There also needs to be a realistic marketing budget to support these activities. After the plan is created, they should constantly revisit it and make changes as necessary. It should contain both short-term and long-term goals, both of which should be realistic. It is also important for marketers to constantly evaluate the success of marketing activities by finding out return on investment. They should try to measure as many of the activities as possible to evaluate where the money is best spent.

## Marketing strategies

There are a variety of marketing strategies a business can employ. With an undifferentiated marketing strategy, the company has the same marketing strategy and marketing mix (product, placement, promotion, and price) for the whole target market. It doesn't differentiate between anyone. This can be easier and less expensive because the company just needs one campaign, but it can also be less effective because the segments in markets differ in tastes and responses to marketing. They might benefit from different strategies. In a differentiated marketing strategy, the company divides the target market into segments based on similar characteristics and creates a marketing mix and strategy for each segment. Although more expensive, it can be more efficient. A third option is a concentrated marketing strategy in which a business focuses only on one segment of the target market and markets towards them. Again, they only need one plan, but they are risking everything on one market and are possibly ignoring other potential customers.

## Competitive marketing strategies

A company can choose from one of many penetration strategies to get sales from competitors. They may try price adjustments by lowering prices. They can increase the amount of promotion with an effort like an advertising campaign. They can try different distribution channels to make it easier for consumers to get their products. They can also improve the product so that more people are interested in it and start to prefer it to competitors' products. Another type of marketing strategy is horizontal diversification. The company produces products that are different than its current offerings, but which might be desired by their current market. They might be able to increase sales this way and still target the same market.

## Market segmentation

Market segmentation involves breaking up a large target market into segments to try to find an ideal group to target. There are various ways a company can segment the market, including by the population's demographics; the physical location of the population; and psychographic characteristics such as lifestyles, values, attitudes, personalities, social class, and interests.

Segments need to be measurable, of enough size to generate a profit, stable, convenient to reach, and made of people who prefer the same products. Once a company has segmented the market, they may choose a concentration or multi-segment strategy. In a concentration strategy, the company chooses one segment to pursue. This will be good for a company that has a specific product that would appeal to one group. For instance, a very expensive car company such as Ferrari only focuses on people who choose to drive very expensive cars. The brand does not offer cheaper cars because they want their brand to be known as an ultra-luxury brand. With a multi-segment strategy, companies market to more than one segment and may change the marketing mix accordingly. More sales can be achieved because there are more possible customers.

## Factors that influence decisions in marketing

Business ethics should be considered during the decision making process. Marketers have to be sure not to do something unethical when marketing or they can get in trouble with consumers. Sociocultural factors also affect marketing. Different cultures respond to different types of marketing. Marketers should take advantage of the technology available. For instance, many utilize social media because it is inexpensive and wide-reaching. Of course, marketers have to follow laws and regulations or they could be subject to fines or other penalizations. Marketers evaluate the market and use different methods to forecast sales to help them make marketing decisions. For instance, they may perform trend analysis to find patterns in sales data to get an idea of future sales. They can use that to evaluate past marketing strategies and help create the best ones for the future.

## Product life cycle

A new product has a life cycle, characterized by introduction, growth, maturity, and decline. In the introduction stage, the goal is to make people aware of the product and create a market. There are different pricing strategies such as penetration pricing or high skim pricing. The company brands it and promotes to early adopters. In the growth stage, the company tries to get more market share. Promotions work to get consumers to prefer the product over other offerings. They may add new features to the product or add new types of distribution. It will be promoted to more people. Once a product reaches maturity, the sales growth decreases as competition may arise, causing a possible lower price. The company works to keep the market share it has as well as maintain its profit. They may improve the product to make it more differentiated and work to promote these differences to consumers. In the decline stage, sales decline. Companies may choose to keep the product with or without changes, harvest it with lowered costs, or discontinue it.

## Product lines and product mixes

A product line is a group of related products a company offers. They may be related by price, function, target market, or other characteristics. A product mix comprises all the products a company offers. Its width refers to the number of product lines with it, its length covers the amount of products in a line, its depth covers the amount of versions of the same product there are, and its consistency refers to the uniformity of those versions. There are various factors that influence decisions on product lines and product mix. Companies should consider how much products cost to make and their sales potential. They need to consider what products their target buyers will purchase. If there is a reason their main products won't sell, they might need to develop new products. Additionally, if a product is older, they may want to add new features to entice people to stay with it. Companies are constantly changing their product mix and lines.

## Branding

Branding is very important for a company to make its product known in the market. It is how the company distinguishes its product or products as differentiated and may include logos, names, graphics, shapes, and more. It can help its product stand out and build loyalty to it, especially as it matures. There are different types of branding strategies. Sometimes they use company branding, where the brand is connected with the general company but not individual product, such as Rolex Watches. Sometimes the name of a product is important such as Hershey's Kisses. Attitude branding involves connecting the product with a feeling. They may successfully connect the product to happiness, for instance. In iconic branding, the brand helps with the person's identity. This would be a very well-known name brand such as Apple. With a no-brand strategy, the packaging is simple as if there is no brand. In the others, the labels and packaging can go a long way in promoting the brand. For instance, an expensive watch will generally be packaged nicely and elegantly. Brands are a very valuable intangible asset.

## Distribution channels and channel integration

Many companies use intermediaries to make the flow of products more effective and efficient. A direct channel takes the product straight from the producer to the consumer. This might be a face-to-face sale or an online sale. An indirect channel takes it through nonaffiliated retailers, wholesalers, or other parties. It may be a one-level channel with one intermediary such as a retailer, a two level channel with a wholesaler and retailer, or more levels. Some companies take advantage of horizontal or vertical integration. Horizontal integration happens when a company attains a similar company. A company that owns a popular website might take over another, for instance. In vertical integration, a company will also own another part of the production and/or distribution process. For instance, a company that makes chocolate chip cookies takes over a firm that makes chocolate chips or opens a bakery to sell their cookies. Exclusive distribution channels have very few intermediaries; selective distribution has a few; and in intensive distribution, the products are located in many outlets.

## Parts of a distribution system

A distribution system involves getting a product from the production line to the customer. It contains various parts. First is order processing, in which the consumer places an order that translates to the purchased products. It is important that this be both efficient and accurate. Next is materials handling, which is all of the processes involved with caring for, storing, and moving the materials of production and products. With inventory management, companies strive to keep the cost of inventory as low as possible while increasing the quality of the products. A good system can reduce costs significantly. Many companies warehouse products and need to find ways to make that as efficient as possible to reduce costs. Finally, transportation must be done to get the finished goods to consumers as quickly and inexpensively as possible. Technology has helped distribution systems a great deal. One example is using bar codes so a company can always know where a product is. Many computerized systems run parts of the distribution system.

## Retailers

Mass merchandisers are large retail stores that sell many different types of products. They may sell anything from furniture to clothing to appliances, all in the same store. Sears is an example of a mass merchandiser. Discount stores such as Wal-Mart generally sell items at lower price points than other sources. Many times the quality is less. Many people like to buy at chain stores. These are stores that have similar locations in different places. People like shopping at familiar places because they are accustomed to them and feel comfortable in them. They know what to expect. Specialty stores specialize in a specific type of product and related goods. For instance, a small store that sells only bath and body items may be a specialty store. These sometimes offer higher prices, but employees will often have more knowledge of the items the store sells. Supermarkets specialize in all types of foods and drinks.

## Factors that affect retailing choices

One factor that affects what retailers a business chooses for its products is store location. A company should make sure the store is located in a place convenient to its market. The product mix also plays a factor. A company may want to look for a store that offers products that will aid in sales of its own products. For instance, a toy manufacturer will want to target toy stores where people are specifically going to shop for toys. The atmosphere also plays a part. The company will want the atmosphere to match the product. For instance, a company that manufactures high-end clothing may look for an exclusive boutique to sell their products. How the product will be displayed matters. Products that are displayed to stand out, such as the books that are on a special table at a bookstore, will garner more attention and sell better. Companies may look for these opportunities. All of these factors play a part in retailing choices.

## Stages consumers use to make decisions and factors that affect decision making

Many consumers go through a process when deciding to make a purchase. First they may recognize a need such as a need for a new car. Next, they will search for information such as information on the new models. After that, they will evaluate the different alternatives such as looking at the prices and features of the models. They will make a decision on whether to purchase and what to purchase. Afterwards, they will evaluate their purchase and whether it met their expectations. Various factors affect decision making, including cultures, society, personal factors (how easily the person spends), and demographics. Various adverting strategies try to entice buyers at a specific decision-making spot such as a call to action or information when someone is comparison shopping. There are many motives behind making a purchase. Some people buy emotionally—i.e., a new dress that a girl doesn't need but which makes her feel like a princess. Some are physical and others rational, like a basic car to fulfill basic needs. Different marketing strategies are made to fulfill different needs.

## Selling process

The selling process is made of a number of steps. First is prospecting, or the process of looking for new customers. Sellers should consider existing customers and their traits as well as where new customers might be. The pre-approach is researching and understanding potential customers. If a seller knows what the customer is looking for, he will be able to give the best sales pitch. The approach is the start of the relationship and is crucial because it will identify the seller as someone a buyer isn't interested in or somebody with something to offer. The seller must engage the person and come off as knowledgeable and able and willing to help. The presentation should be based on how the product will benefit the buyer. It's not just that a dress is beautiful, but that the dress will make the buyer beautiful. In the closing, the salesperson strives to effectively move it to a sale. They figure out what needs to happen to have the customer agree to the sale. Finally, the follow-up can help sustain a relationship and keep repeat customers. The car salesman might call the customer to ask how he likes his new car.

- 71 -

## Sales support, order taking, and creative selling

There are many processes that are related to the sales process that can make a large difference in the success of selling. Sales support provides support services to salespeople. They may monitor the accounts of customers, gather data that is useful to the salespeople, answer the phone, work on scheduling, process sales leads, manage sales targets, and help with correspondence between sales team and customers. Some people just perform order taking. They do not attempt to convince anyone to buy but instead just take the orders. In creative selling, the salesperson follows a step-by-step process to engage the customer and hopefully secure the sale.

## Factors that influence customer satisfaction

Customer service is one factor that influences customer satisfaction. Customers want to feel like there is someone easily accessible to contact if something goes wrong and that the company hears their concerns and responds appropriately to the situation. Companies with good customer service will often be able to retain a customer even after a problem as compared to a company with poor customer service. Many companies focus on relationship marketing. They strive to form a relationship with the customer. They may provide more personalized service or reach out to customers. The customers will feel more valued. They may strive to increase customer satisfaction. Of course customer satisfaction is influenced by the quality of the product as well as efficient service. They do not want to feel cheated by the company; instead they want to feel like they're purchasing from a responsible company that cares about its customers. Companies that get satisfied customers will see more repeat customers.

## Douglas McGregor's Theory X Assumptions

Douglas McGregor's Theory X focuses on three main assumptions regarding employee motivation and behavior.  First, one must assume that employees, by their inborn nature, do not like to work and will try to do as little as possible. This leads to a management style in which a supervisor has no choice but to manage in a dictatorial manner, using coercion, strict control, direction, and threats in order to persuade the employee to actually work. It assumes money as the sole motivating factor for employees and that only great incentives or strict punishments will be effective in convincing an employee to work. It also assumes the person does not possess ambition and wishes for this direction, desiring security first and foremost. Furthermore, it assumes employees worry only about themselves and that the manager must assume control to get the most out of his or her employees.

## Douglas McGregor's Theory Y Assumptions

Douglas McGregor's Theory Y provides a positive view of employees. It assumes that employees can be self-motivated and enjoy work just like they might enjoy play. It is natural to them. Although their talents are often under-utilized, most people do possess the talent, skills, imagination, ingenuity, creativity, and motivation to solve problems and direct themselves. They can control themselves, and accept and even search for responsibility and work to accomplish goals on their own. They desire success at work for the inherent satisfaction of performing well. Managers need not exercise strict control to force employees to work, but should instead organize, arrange, and allow for decision making in employees. These assumptions lead to a culture where supervisors work with employees and allow for positive communication and employee development.

## Management methods

### Total quality management

Total quality management is a management method that strives for better internal processes and increased customer satisfaction. If done correctly, costs can be lowered, performance will be raised, and customers will be more pleased. There are various principles of total quality management. First, managers need to believe they can and should manage quality levels. If there is a problem, it is rooted in the process, not the employees. Instead of focusing on fixing just the symptoms, managers should look for the cure to what's really wrong. Quality is the job of every employee at the company. There must be a way to measure quality so a company can understand its position. The company should always work on improving quality. Quality investing is long-term; it can take a while, but the resulting success can also be long term.

### Management by objectives

First coined in 1954 in Peter Drucker's "The Practice of Management," management by objectives (MBO) is a management model that focuses on the creation of objectives or goals. A key component of MBO is that both managers and employees create the objectives. The employees will then be more motivated to achieve them because they had a say in their formulation. In addition to making objectives, companies must formulate a way to measure performance to ascertain whether the objectives are being met. An advantage of MBO is that it can produce a better relationship between management and employees, as well as more employee commitment. A disadvantage is that its focus on end results rather than on forming a comprehensive plan may make it more difficult to reach the results.

### Activity-based management

In activity-based management, managers examine activities to evaluate costs and value added. The goal is to eliminate or improve the activities that are not as valuable to the company. Managers look at overhead costs and try to allocate resources to where they will be the most valuable. One disadvantage to activity-based management is that some activities that do not show an obvious financial benefit may still have intrinsic value. For instance, if a company spends money on a luxurious work environment, this may not be obvious in a dollar amount gain. However, if it helps them attract higher quality workers who will be more effective, then it will produce financial results, even if they aren't easily measured. Companies use the information to make better decisions.

## Functions of management

Managers perform many different roles, and Henri Fayol created a list of five basic management functions, four of which are generally identified today. These include planning, organizing, leading, and controlling. Planning involves creating a plan of action to accomplish a goal for the organization. For instance, if the manager wishes to increase employee efficiency, then he or she may create a plan to give incentives to top performers. The leader will make a list of logical steps to accomplish the goal. Organizing includes resource distribution as well as organizing employees in the best way to carry out the plan. For instance, the manager will decide which employees can help with the plan. He or she might delegate work and direct employees to help implement it. When a manager is leading, he or she connects with the employees personally. He or she might inspire, motivate, and encourage. The employees should look up to the manager as a leader. Controlling occurs after the plan has been implemented. Managers evaluate whether the goals of the plan have been met. If not, he or she will take action to reach the goal.

<u>Planning</u>
One of the most important jobs of a manager is the planning function. Managers need to formulate detailed plans to reach their goals. They need to carefully design the steps that will reach these goals. These steps should be flexible, as they may need to change as the plan is brought to fruition. There are different types of plans within an organization. A strategic plan deals with the company as a whole and is long term. It might be related to the objectives and vision for the business. A tactical plan outlines the tactics the company will utilize to fulfill the strategic plan. An operational plan deals with the daily running of the company. In this type of plan, short-term objectives are highlighted. Managers that plan well have a better chance of realizing their goals.

<u>Organizing</u>
Once a manager has created a plan to reach a goal, the next step in management is organizing. This is an extremely critical step. In this step, managers must decide how to allocate the resources they have to best achieve their goals. For instance, a manager may decide how much money each department gets. Another important part of organizing is researching the talents and abilities of employees and delegating the work in a way to best take advantage of their skills. Managers will decide who will fill each role and how the work will be done. He (or she) must also make sure employees understand these roles and can accomplish them. The manager must also dictate how decisions are made and by whom, conduct problem solving, and create the chain of command and communication procedures. He should decide who has managerial power and how reporting will occur. Authority is often delegated to increase efficiency. Once organizing is complete, there should be an organizational structure that dictates the roles, power, responsibility, and information distribution.

<u>Controlling</u>
Once a manager has created a plan, organized, and led it, he must perform the fourth and final management function—controlling. This is the process by which a manager evaluates the results of a plan to ascertain whether it has met his goals. When controlling, the manager must first decide how he (or she) will measure performance. For instance, if the goal is increased financial position, he might look at profits. Other common goals might involve efficiency, production, or customer satisfaction. Next, he will need to develop a way to measure this. He might look at sales data, customer satisfaction surveys, or production numbers. The data should be clear, objective, and measureable. Next, the manager will evaluate the new numbers compared to standards. For instance, he might look at customer satisfaction numbers this year as compared to the year before the plan. Did satisfaction increase as he'd predicted? Finally, he will decide whether corrective action is needed, then plan and take it if necessary. For instance, if customer satisfaction did not go up as he had hoped, he will investigate to see what happened and decide how to change the plan to reach his goals.

**Levels of management**

Many companies have different levels of management, and each level is responsible for certain functions. Managers are typically broken into top-level management, middle-level management, and low-level management. The top level managers are the managers in charge of running the organization as a whole and making the major decisions for the company. They oversee everything about the company and control it. They generally have the most experience, with skills in leadership, delegation, and making major decisions. The CEO and president are examples of top-level management. Middle-level managers bring organizational plans to fruition. They are delegated some authority and are a liaison between top-level management and low-level management. They will often have a decent amount of experience and are adept at solving problems, building teams, and developing talent. A department manager or general manager of a store is an example of middle management. Low-level managers spend their time leading, directing, and supervising employees. Employees can go to them with problems. They typically have more skills and experience than general employees, and they should be good at dealing with people. Examples include foremen and supervisors.

## Leadership styles

In an authoritarian (autocratic) leadership style, the rules and regulations are strict and the manager keeps firm control. The relationship is purely professional, and there is a lot of supervision. Problems can occur when employees become unhappy that their ideas and suggestions are not heard. A democratic (participative) leadership style is very popular. The manager does not make all the decisions, but instead shares them with the group. There is discussion and debate, and the employees are encouraged to provide ideas, which can contribute to the group. There is still guidance and the leader makes the ultimate decisions, but everyone helps throughout the process. Employees are often happy with this type of management. With a paternalistic leadership style, the manager acts almost as a parent and the employees as children who trust and are loyal to their leader. They follow his (or her) lead. The laissez-faire (delegative) style of leadership is one in which the workers make all the decisions without any managerial control. This can be problematic if the workers cease to become productive because no one is holding them responsible.

## SWOT analysis

SWOT refers to strengths, weaknesses, opportunities, and threats. A SWOT analysis is a powerful tool that allows managers to evaluate both internal factors and the outside environment with the goal of making the best business decisions. A company may produce a chart to illustrate the SWOT analysis. They will list strengths such as positive assets, a good work force, etc. Next to strengths, weaknesses such as financial limitations or government regulations that limit the company will be listed. Next, the company will look at opportunities such as increasing demand for a product. They will then look for threats such as a competitor's new patent. Once the company has identified as many of these as possible, managers will look to take advantage of the strengths and opportunities, minimize the weaknesses, and turn the threats into opportunities. For instance, if the threat to a cookie company is that people are more health conscious, the company may turn the threat into an opportunity by producing a healthier cookie. By understanding these factors, the company can take advantage of what it has and address the problem areas.

## Types of financing businesses may utilize

When large companies want money for short term debt obligations, they may give out commercial paper, a money-market security. This can be sold to a dealer and then to the market, or straight to a buy and hold investor. It does not cost as much as credit within a bank. It is not secured, and the maturity is between one and 364 days. Businesses can also get a long-term loan to finance their business. A number of banks and organizations offer loans. Rates and amounts vary. A business can also issue stock to raise money. This is essentially selling a small piece of ownership in a company. Many businesses use a combination of these strategies.

## Time value of money

Because money has the ability to earn interest, the present value of money is worth more than the same amount of money in the future. For instance, the $100 an individual receives today is worth more than the same $100 he receives in one year. That is because he will be able to earn interest on the money he receives today and turn it into more money in the future. The sooner he receives the money, the more it is worth. The future value of money depends on the interest rate. For instance, if a person has $100 now and the interest rate is 10 percent, he will have $110 in one year. This can be calculated with the algebraic formula: $PV = FV / (1 + r)$ in which PV is the present value, FV is future value and r is the interest rate. In this case, it would be $100 = 110 / (1 + 0.1)$. This formula can also be used to calculate missing values.

## Budget types

A sales budget is a budget that shows the expected sales for a period of time. This is shown in units and dollars and is often categorized by product categories or geographic location. A production budget, typically seen in a "push" manufacturing system, shows the amount of products that should be made. The sales forecast and finished goods inventory are used to calculate this. A cash budget covers the inflows and outflows of cash that are expected. The four sections of a cash budget are receipts, financing, disbursements, and cash surplus or deficit. A capital expenditure budget covers investments in long-term projects and capital assets. Generally it is for a time span of three to 10 years and may cover investments in buildings, land, plants, and equipment.

## Master budget

A master budget encompasses all of the budgets of a company to give an entire view of the business as a whole, allowing for comprehensive financial planning. It has two major components: the operating budget and the financial budget. The operating budget is created first because the financial budget will depend on its numbers. The operating budget includes the sales budget, production budget, direct materials purchases budget, direct labor budget, overhead budget, selling and administrative expenses budget, and cost of goods manufactured budget. The financial budget contains a schedule of expected cash receipts from customers, a schedule of expected cash payments of suppliers, the cash budget, a budgeted income statement, and a budgeted balance sheet.

## Budgeting approaches

With a zero-base budget, the managers first decide on the outcome they want, then create the expenditures to make that happen. The budget needs to match the outcome. This is often used for governments and other service-level entities so that the desired outcomes are achieved. With flexible budgeting, varying sales levels are put into the model, and the planned expense levels change accordingly. This can be advantageous when the company has trouble predicting sales. In a static budget the expenditures do not change in response to sales levels. This is often used for public entities with fixed grants. With top-down budgeting, the top management makes the budget for the firm as a whole and decides on all the allocations. The lower levels do not get a say in what they get. With bottom-up budgeting, the lower level managers have a chance to participate and help set their own budget needs. Those are then put together to formulate the budget of the company as a whole.

## Cost-benefit analysis

A cost-benefit analysis is an important process to complete when making decisions in business. It is a way of looking objectively at all the costs and benefits of different options to make the best decision for the company. First, the company must decide on the different options available. Once it has the options, a cost-benefit analysis should be run on each. The company should compile all the costs of an option, being careful to not omit important factors such as overhead costs, costs of operation, and opportunity costs. It is important to measure in objective terms such as money. Next, all the benefits should be compiled. Benefits affecting the employees, company, customers, and all stakeholders should be considered. The time value of money should also be applied so values are accurate. The company will then compare the costs and benefits to see what the net benefit (or cost) of each option would be. The company can then move forward with best strategy.

**Production methods**

Continuous processes
A continuous processes production system is a method of production in which products are continually produced. This is advantageous when a great volume of products are needed. Businesses use this for products such as cars, paper products, and many food products. The production line may have a significant amount of machinery to make it semi-automated. People generally control the computers with a workforce that may be a combination of skilled and unskilled laborers. The production is steady and will continuously run at all times unless there is a maintenance break. There is less flexibility with this type of production and it can cost a lot of money to set up, but then the cost per item can be lower as there is less need for labor. There are typically numerous quality control measures, such as sampling, to ensure quality.

Batch operations
With a batch operations production method, similar items are made together in batches. They proceed together through each stage of production and then all move to the next stage. An example is a bakery producing batches of cookies, desserts, or pastries. Advantages are that each batch can be customized—they can make one batch of chocolate chip cookies and another of oatmeal to suit customer needs. Also, it saves money and time to make them in batches as compared to doing them individually. Companies can save money by using the same production systems on more than one product. Also, many companies could not afford the expensive equipment needed for a continuous production method. It is a suitable method when companies don't know how many of a product they'll need, as well as for seasonal items. One disadvantage is that companies may have some downtime as they go from one batch to another. Another disadvantage is that companies need to have raw materials for different products in stock.

**Inventory systems**

Traditional
A traditional inventory system involves ordering materials and storing them until they are needed. Companies may make agreements with suppliers to receive volume discounts. There will also be extra inventory on hand in case demand suddenly goes up, and a brief interruption in delivery will not halt the entire system. There are also disadvantages to this type of system. Generally it is not as efficient as a just-in-time system. Companies have to pay for the cost of storing the materials, which can be substantial. They could also potentially be stuck with extra materials if they ultimately do not need as many as they predicted. Companies should weigh the advantages and disadvantages when deciding which is best for them.

JIT
A just-in-time (JIT) inventory system is an inventory system in which materials come in just as they are needed for production. The idea is to keep inventory as low as possible, thereby lowering the costs of storage. Businesses spend less on carrying costs and can also save with the time value of

money because they do not have to pay for materials until they need them. They will not end up with extra materials that go to waste. One consideration with this system is that companies need to be able to forecast the amount of materials they will need. They will not have extras on hand, so if there is a sudden increase in demand, they may not have the materials available to meet that demand. Also, if there is a problem with materials, they will not have any extras on hand to cushion them.

## Organization structures of companies

Functional structures, team structures, and adaptive structures
Companies can be structured in a variety of ways, and each type possesses its own advantages and disadvantages. A company with a functional structure organizes the employees, tasks, and supervision in the company by function. For instance, there will be a marketing department, a production department, etc. The advantage is that these functions can become highly specialized. A disadvantage is that it can hamper communication between the different departments. Companies that make a lot of standardized products may use this type of structure. A team structure is where people with different abilities are put together to build teams that can achieve more than the individuals alone. The teams can be flexible and draw on the strengths of the members. An adaptive structure has multifunctional teams instead of a rigid hierarchy. All levels are encouraged to contribute to give the most to the organization. This flexibility can be beneficial, but it may also be more difficult to manage.

Networks, matrix structures, and product-based structures
There are various organizational structures a company can utilize, and the best one depends on the characteristics of the business. One type is a network structure. In this structure, business functions that can be accomplished with less cost and/or better quality by others are outsourced. Managers dedicate a lot of time to dealing with these external forces. For instance, a clothing company may find a company that can make the goods with fewer resources, allowing the main company to focus on other functions. In a matrix structure, employees are grouped by function and product for maximum efficiency. Teams are often employed. For instance, if a company sells both cars and boats, they might have a car sales department and a boat sales department. In a product-based structure, the company is organized by product. A grocery store will have a produce section, a meat section, a dairy section, etc. This is often used for larger companies.

Centralized and decentralized structures
In centralized structures, one individual makes decisions for the company, whereas in decentralized structures, there is a team and the decisions are made at different levels. Which structure is best for the business depends on the manager, size, and other factors. Centralized structures allow for quick decisions and efficiency because only one person is making the decisions. Decentralized structures allow multiple individuals to contribute, which can be slower, but can also provide more information, insight, and ideas to the organization. Some centralized organizations have a lot of bureaucracy, which can slow things down, or they might inadvertently make decisions that are not the best for the lower levels. Decentralized structures sometimes struggle with too many differing opinions. Each method has its advantages and disadvantages.

Formal and informal structures
The formal structure is the exact chain of leadership and the formal hierarchy. It will start with the owner or CEO and then work its way down the chain of command with clear indications of who is in charge. The informal structure is often centered on project groups or even on friendship. Those who are more knowledgeable or just more natural leaders may take on that informal role, even

without specific authority. Others might look to him (or her) for guidance because he knows more, is more willing to help or provides other leadership functions. The response may be quicker and more efficient. Both structures are utilized in many businesses.

## Staffing process

Planning stage
It is important for human resource personnel to properly plan the staffing process. First, they need to perform human resources audits. This is the process in which all the functions, policies, and characteristics of a company's human resources department are examined to look for problems, find best practices, and increase efficacy and efficiency. It is also done to make sure practices properly protect the company legally and effectively. The company will then perform a job analysis to look at a job to understand all of its functions and attributes as well as those needed of the employee who will perform the job. Next, human resource employees can create a job description with specifications on what needs to be done and who could do it. They can then start to look for the employee. Sometimes they look inwards. Succession planning is the process of looking at existing employees and planning and preparing them to move up in the company to leadership positions. It can make things move more smoothly when the company grows or a key person leaves.

Staffing procedures
There are a number of staffing procedures companies must perform. First, they must recruit potential employees. This can be done in a number of ways. They may send out job advertisements or contact a recruiting agency. They can go to job fairs. Once they have an employee, the company must train him (or her). They must have a good training program that prepares him to do his job satisfactorily. The company must also evaluate its employees. Many companies formally evaluate employees on an annual basis, but in reality, employees are constantly evaluated for performance. The company can help employees to improve themselves. Evaluations can be used as a basis for raises. At times, employees need to be terminated. This can be because of a company situation, or due to the fault of the employee. Procedures should be put in place so this is as smooth as possible for both the employee and company. With the right procedures in place, the company will run more efficiently.

## Addressing diversity in the workplace

It is important for businesses to embrace and promote diversity. People from different backgrounds have different ideas and can contribute in many positive ways. Companies should make sure that there is diversity at their office and no unfair hiring practices. Many companies make a concerted effort to hire people from all different backgrounds. In the office, it is vital to promote an atmosphere of acceptance and tolerance. There should be a zero-tolerance policy for discrimination of any type. This should be communicated to employees regularly. Avenues should be provided to report any problems. With diligence, every workplace can celebrate and enjoy the benefits of diversity.

## Cross-training

Cross-training is when employees are trained to perform functions outside of the typical functions of their job. For instance, someone who works in the copywriting department of a firm might spend a little time in the graphic design department. There are various advantages to cross-training. First, if an employee is absent, someone else may be able to take over without a problem. It can ensure that the job functions are completed even when someone is absent. It can also help a person better do his or her job. For instance, the copywriter who learns about graphic design might get a better idea of how his or her copy is going to look as a whole. Employees might also be able to communicate better with other departments when they understand more of what they are doing. Additionally, it can promote teamwork and help motivate employees because it helps them to better understand the company. Employees who are cross-trained are easier to promote because they already understand multiple parts of the company and the organization as a whole, which is an advantage for both the company and employee.

## Maslow's hierarchy of needs

In his work on human motivation, Abraham Maslow created Maslow's hierarchy of needs, a five-tiered approach to needs and motivation. The pyramid-shaped hierarchy places basic needs at the bottom, which must be attained before higher levels are reached. The desire for these needs will increase the longer they are denied. The bottom level of the pyramid encompasses physiological needs. These are what a human needs to survive such as food, water, air, and sleep. The need for security comes next. These include important needs such as the desire for a safe home, medical care, and a secure job. Once these are achieved, a person moves on to social needs. People want love, affection, and belonging though friends, social involvement, and romance. The next tier is esteem needs. These make a person feel like they are worthwhile. People look for a sense of accomplishment and recognition from others. Once a person has achieved these four basic needs, they can progress to the growth need, the top tier of self-actualization. This is where people have enjoyed personal growth and are reaching their potential. They do not worry as much about others' opinions and instead focus on their own growth.

## Collective bargaining

Collective bargaining occurs when a company's management engages in talks with representatives of a workforce (often a trade union). They discuss numerous aspects of the business and its labor including working conditions, pay, hours, benefits, and more. It is advantageous to employees because they can have more bargaining power and more of a say when they band together. It is advantageous for the company because they just negotiate with one group and can get everything arranged and set without needing to go through the same process with numerous employees numerous times. It avoids many future problems and arguments. Collective bargaining is commonly seen in many different industries and fields.

## Conflict resolution strategies

When conflict occurs in the workplace, efficiency and efficacy can be impacted, thus it is important to employ conflict resolution strategies. There are numerous strategies a company can utilize. First, the company should address the situation right away. Small conflicts can grow into large ones with time. The manager should talk to the parties separately to get their side of the story. Sometimes the conflict is more of a misunderstanding than anything, and it can be simply solved by understanding the two points of view. The manager should understand what each person wants and see if there is a way to compromise and make everyone happy. They can try to mediate between the two people, allowing each party to speak. This meeting should be civil, calm, and constructive. Managers should try to come up with a solution that is beneficial for everyone, trying to make everyone happy (if possible) when it ends. If necessary, a follow-up should occur.

## Effects of group dynamics on individual behavior

People can behave differently when in a group, and how groups act is an area of study called group dynamics. It is important for managers to understand these forces so they can promote positive behavior. Groupthink is a negative behavior that occurs when the people in a group want harmony so much that they minimize opposing viewpoints. They make a decision without considering all of the alternatives because the people do not want conflict. Some people feel a loyalty to others. Also, they may have the mistaken impression that others agree it can't be wrong, even if many are harboring their own doubts. It is important to avoid this. Sometimes there can be conflict in a group and this can prevent the group from making decisions. Groups can also be good, especially if there is group cohesion, where people feel good about each other. If people are encouraged to speak their minds, then new opinions can emerge and the group can make the best decision possible.

## Organizational culture and subculture within the workplace

Corporate culture encompasses many facets, including values, traditions, and customs. For instance, there may be a formal culture in which people dress formally and address each other in a formal manner. There might be a very polite culture in which people try to be very kind to each other. Management plays a big part in making the culture, which can have a large effect on the work that gets done. Within this culture, there are also subcultures that may be very unique. For instance, the computer department in a firm may have a different subculture than the rest of the company, formed by their shared values, interests, etc. The various subcultures can affect the organization's culture as a whole. A positive culture can have a positive effect on the company.

## Strategies to promote teamwork

Employees must work together even with differing and (at times) conflicting personalities. There are different measures employers can take to promote teamwork. One method is to incorporate team-building exercising. These might involve games or fun activities. There are companies that perform team-building sessions for companies. They can help employees get to know each other better and learn how to work together. There should be rules for teams to promote respect. For instance, employees should never insult others at the office. Employers should make sure employees adhere to the rules. If there is one person who is a problem, then management should talk to that person to address the situation. Recognition of teams is another way to promote teamwork. A company can recognize groups that work well together and accomplish their goals. The team members should have clear roles. This can help stop disagreements from a misunderstanding of roles and responsibilities. With strong teamwork comes better efficiency and productivity.

## Influences on employees' morale and motivation

First, employees should be fairly compensated. Employees who are underpaid may feel cheated and not motivated. Likewise, if a person is overworked, he or she will feel less motivated at the job. Jobs that allow the workers some flexibility can promote motivation. Also, workers who feel appreciated and valued have higher morale and motivation. Companies can accomplish this by praising employees or having recognition programs such as an employee-of-the-month program. Workers also like to have some say or responsibility in their work rather than just being told what to do. Workers will also feel more motivated and have higher morale in a positive culture where people are respectful of each other. The working conditions affect employee motivation; employees will not feel very motivated if they are in a hot room with 10 other people. The ability of the boss to lead well and create a good atmosphere also affects employee attitudes. Companies should work hard to control these factors to promote high morale and motivation.

## Promoting job satisfaction among employees

If possible, employers can increase satisfaction by being flexible in employee schedules. When workers do not feel overworked, they are happier. Also, workers like to feel satisfied at their job—delegating some responsibility and letting them contribute instead of dictating every move can promote job satisfaction. Employers should be respectful of employees and provide a professional culture. Employees do not want to be talked down to or treated as if they are inferior. Employers can show that they care about employees. It can be as simple as a manager recognizing when an employee is going through a difficult time, or offering a reward for a success. Employees like to be recognized for their hard work. Allowing employees to grow and feel like they are contributing is important. People will also be more satisfied if there is a place they can go with their complaints. It is worthwhile for a company to spend the time, effort, and money to promote job satisfaction. With higher satisfaction comes increased productivity.

## Pertinent factors when determining compensation

First, the company should consider the experience the employee possesses. An individual with 10 years of experience is generally more valuable than an employee directly out of college; he (or she) will expect and deserve higher compensation. The years the employee has been with the company also affects compensation. Many companies give a raise every year to reflect cost of living, merit, or both. Skills should also be considered. An employee with better or rarer skills should be compensated for them. The education of the employee matters. Generally, the higher the degree, the greater the compensation. Companies may have a salary range for the position based upon the wages paid for similar people in similar companies. This will depend on location and cost of living. Some companies pay a little more to attract higher quality employees or a little less to save money. Also, the company's financial state might affect pay. A company that is doing well will have more cash to spread around while one that is having difficulty might be more frugal. The other types of benefits offered will also affect pay.

## Common benefits employees receive

Employees receive many benefits in addition to financial compensation. Most full-time employees receive some type of paid time off. This may include sick, vacation, and personal days. Often, this number increases depending on the length of time the employee has been with the company. Companies also typically offer time off for holidays such as Thanksgiving and Christmas. The company may offer health insurance plans and even contribute to the premiums. Some employers also offer vision benefits, dental plans, and life insurance plans. Companies also often offer retirement benefits. It might be in the form of a pension, 401(k) plan, or an employee stock plan. The company may contribute to these as well. These benefits can be worth a great deal to an employee.

## Retirement plans

There are different types of retirement plans for which an employee may be eligible. A pension provides a fixed sum on a regular basis to an employee after retirement. This is often given to people who worked in public office or the service. Some employees are also eligible for an employee stock ownership plan (ESOP). In this type of retirement plan, the company puts stock or money for stock into an account on behalf of the employee. This may have to vest over time. The employee does not control the stock directly until he (or she) leaves the firm, and then it is distributed. Many companies offer 401(k) plans. These are tax-advantageous plans that allow people to defer their income taxes, both in earnings and contributions. A lot of employers will match a percentage of the contributions of the employee. A person can also get an individual retirement account that provides tax advantages.

## Managing employee paid time off

Employers give employees paid time off in the form of vacation, sick time, and holidays. Companies may manage these by giving a certain amount of leave for each year of service, an amount that may increase when the person reaches a milestone such as five years. They will often do it as an accrual process, with each pay period showing how much the employee has accrued in time. Companies decide which holidays to give off to employees. Most offer New Years, Thanksgiving Day, Christmas, Independence Day, Labor Day, and Memorial Day, but others also offer days like Veteran's Day and Martin Luther King, Jr. Day. Some companies have decided to combine sick, personal, and vacation time so people can use the time as they wish. People will typically ask for the time off from their managers or the human resources department. Some companies have a computerized system for this, which makes it easier to manage.

## Workers' compensation

Workers' compensation is insurance that companies pay for to protect themselves and their employees. It covers medical expenses and partial salary losses to employees who are hurt while on the job. It does not matter if the person is at fault (i.e., if the person tripped over his own feet), he would still be eligible (although not necessarily if it is intentional or due to drugs or alcohol). The injury must occur while the person is working. Employers pay all costs of the program. There may also be payment for economic loss. In the case of an employee killed while on the job, money may be paid to dependents.

## Unemployment insurance

Unemployment insurance provides benefits for workers who lose their jobs without fault of their own. These programs are usually run by the state and are typically funded by employers through taxes. It does not typically cover the entire salary, but instead a portion of it for a specific amount of time. This limit can be extended at times, especially when the economy is particularly bad. A number of factors determine eligibility into the program. The person must not have done something to lose his job. For example, a person will not get unemployment if he is fired for showing up late to work repeatedly. Also, many states require that the individual search for a job while receiving benefits. He might not be eligible if he is receiving other income. The employee must have been at the job for a certain amount of time before being laid off. It does not count for temporary employees or those who voluntarily quit. The amount is based on what the employee was earning.

## Laws and acts preventing discrimination

A number of laws have been created to prevent and punish discrimination. The Americans with Disabilities Act (ADA) protects those with physical and mental disabilities from discrimination, as well as provides many other protections. Those with disabilities must be reasonably accommodated in a number of areas. For instance, someone can't be fired for having a disability.

The Equal Employment Opportunity Commission (EEOC) forbids discrimination against an employee or job applicant due to color, race, gender, religion, age, disability, national origin, or genetic information. Companies must adhere to this in all practices, including hiring, training, pay, termination, benefits, promotions, and harassment. The Age Discrimination in Employment Act (ADEA) is similar, but forbids discrimination based on a person's age. Strict penalties could be enforced for any parties violating the above laws and acts.

## FMLA

The Family and Medical Leave Act (FMLA) allows employees who are eligible to take up to 12 weeks (per year) of unpaid leave while having their job and group health insurance protected for one of the following reasons. 1) To care for a newborn or child under one year of age. 2) To care for an adopted or foster child with the employee for one year or less. 3) To provide support to a spouse, parent or child with a serious medical issue. 4) To deal with the employee's own health condition that does not allow him (or her) to work. 5) To deal with an eligible exigency due to a parent's, child's, or spouse's position as a covered military member on covered active duty. If the employee is taking time off to care for an injured or ill covered military member (parent, child, spouse, next of kin) then the eligible leave is extended to 26 weeks.

## FICA

The Federal Insurance Contributions Act (FICA) is a law in the United States that requires money be deducted from income to fund Medicare and social security. The social security portion has a maximum while the Medicare part does not. How much is deducted is dependent on the person's income. It is 12.4 percent for social security and 2.9 percent for Medicare. Those who work for someone else will only have to pay for half the FICA amount while their employer will pay the other half. Self-employed individuals pay it all, but can deduct half from their taxes as an expense of the business. There is an additional 0.9 percent Medicare tax for those making over $200,000 annually.

## COBRA

The Consolidated Omnibus Budget Reconciliation Act (COBRA) is an act that allows employees and their spouses, ex-spouses, and dependent children to continue with group health coverage when it would have been otherwise terminated. Various events can trigger this continuing coverage, including the employee losing his job (without major misconduct), a reduction in hours that would result in losing the benefits, the employee's death, divorce or legal separation, a child becoming no longer dependent, and new eligibility for Medicare. The covered individuals may have to pay for the insurance in its entirety, including an additional two percent for administrative fees. State and local governments must adhere to COBRA, as do companies with 20 or more employees. Some states have laws that cover smaller companies. Coverage may be extended for a maximum of 18 to 36 months depending on the qualifying event.

## HIPAA

The Health Insurance Portability and Accountability Act (HIPAA) provides broad protection for American workers concerning the privacy of health insurance. It gives patients and other individuals broad protections for their identifiable health information and limits who can see the information without permission. In addition, those who hold the information, such as doctor's offices, must put in safeguards so it is not accidently seen by unauthorized individuals. It includes medical records, patient/provider conversations, billing information, and other health information.

Parties that must adhere to the rules include health plans, the majority of health care providers and health care clearinghouses, as well as their business associates.

## Safety in the workplace

The government plays a large role in promoting safety in the workplace. The Occupational Safety and Health Act of 1970 was implemented to prevent accidents at work by requiring safe working conditions. The Occupational Safety and Health Administration (OSHA) was formed by the act and gives and enforces rules and regulations about workplace safety. It conducts investigations, takes complaints, and issues fines. It requires employers to clearly label any hazards, create records of injuries and illnesses related to work, do OSHA-required tests such as air sampling and medical tests (depending on the industry), and tell OSHA if a fatality occurs or three workers go to the hospital. There are various requirements by OSHA, including providing employees with protective equipment, preventing exposure to toxic chemicals, adhering to noise restrictions and more. Also, employees can't be discriminated against for making a complaint.

# Professional Business Education

## Business career paths

There are many different career paths one can take in business. One might try a traditional business position in which he (or she) applies for a business job at a company. The person then works his way up through the corporate ladder, either at that job or switching to other companies. Some people prefer an entrepreneurial path. With the Internet and social media, there are numerous ways to start a low-cost business right from the comfort of home. The person might sell something online from a website or an auction site. Some people work in the business world on a freelance basis. Someone might work as a marketing consultant, for instance. This can be a good option for someone who has experience in the field, but wishes to work from home. Some people choose a combination of these options.

## Sources of information about business careers

Business schools can provide a great resource. Students can find out information about the different career choices as well as current trends. Many of the schools have career centers where students can talk to career advisors. Business and trade associations also offer information. These will often have websites that provide information as well as meetings where individuals can network and learn about careers. The Internet provides a wealth of information about business careers. From business websites to free resources, many websites share business career information. Individuals can easily search for their particular interest on a search engine. Government publications also provide information.

## Important characteristics of individuals pursuing a business career

Personal qualities
Individuals pursuing a career in business will find that certain characteristics can help them. For instance, someone in business should have initiative. He (or she) should be able to take steps without direction. A businessman should be dependable. Clients and customers depend on businesses to fulfill their promises, and companies need to be able to rely on their employees. A businessman should be enthusiastic. He can promote his products or offerings better if he is enthusiastic about them. He can motivate others with this enthusiasm. It is also very important for a businessman to be responsible. Colleagues, clients, and customers need to be able to trust that he will do the right thing. He should be competent. He needs to understand his job and be able to perform it well.

Education, experience, and skills
It is important for someone pursuing a business career to have the right education, experience, and skills. The exact experience necessary will depend on the job. Many employers prefer workers to have a college degree in business or a related field. A Masters of Business Administration (MBA) is very useful for those looking to get ahead in business. Individuals can go beyond that to a doctoral degree, but that is not nearly as common for those not in the education or research field. The more business experience, the better. Even those who haven't had a full-time job may have experience from an internship, part-time job, or apprenticeship. A professional business organization can provide some of this experience as well as information. Someone pursuing a business job should have the ability to do the job effectively as well as reliability, responsibility, enthusiasm, and good

communication skills. He should also have soft skills, the skills related to a person's emotional intelligence quotient such as an ability to be friendly and work well with others.

## Employee rights in business

There are a number of health and safety rights covered under the Occupational Safety and Health Act (OSHA). Employees should work in a safe environment with the proper safety precautions. Employees also have the right to equal employment opportunities. For instance, a person cannot be discriminated against because of gender, race, or religion. A person has the right to earn a fair minimum wage. He (or she) cannot be forced to work for less than that. Workers with disabilities and those in the military have special rights. Workers also receive rights from the Family and Medical Leave Act. For instance, eligible employees can get unpaid but protected leave for the birth of a child or to care for a sick family member. The exact rights range based upon the eligibility requirements, state, and position.

## Strategies to work effectively with business colleagues

Certain strategies help businessmen work well with colleagues. First, it is important for a person to be responsible and reliable. Co-workers become resentful when they can't rely on someone, especially when it reflects on them. Businessmen should practice active listening. People appreciate those who really listen to them, and everyone can get their ideas heard. When a person communicates, he (or she) should do so in a constructive fashion. He should stay positive to the extent possible and explain himself instead of just dictating. He should not be insulting and should keep professional at all times. He should not gossip or insult. He should work to compromise with co-workers and show that he is willing to be flexible. He can help other workers and go above and beyond; people appreciate this and will often pay kind co-workers back with the same courtesy. He should try to solve problems. He should make sure to "pull his own weight" as workers can be resentful if someone is not doing his share. He should work to solve problems and not make them. All of these can make a huge difference in professional relations.

## Career planning strategies to reach career goals

The first step in career planning is to create goals. These should include both short-term and long-term goals. Students should be realistic. They should consider the type of career that would suit them. They should evaluate themselves as far as their abilities, skills, and characteristics to find jobs that would suit them. There are many career assessment tools available at career centers, in books, and online. Of course, most people want to enjoy work; they should consider the types of things they enjoy and look for a job that encompasses that. They should also consider both what they want from and what they want to give to a job. For instance, they should consider the salary they desire as well as the hours they are willing to put in to get it. Students should consider what needs to be done to get their desired job such as further education, work experience, and so forth. They should formulate a plan for how they will climb the ladder toward the ultimate goal and the steps along the way.

## Steps in career planning

Career planning involves a variety of steps to increase an individual's chances of attaining a desired career. First, a person must do a personal assessment. He (or she) should consider his strengths, weaknesses, and abilities as well as his likes and dislikes. He should think about what he wants in a career such as salary, working hours, conditions, and other specifics. Next, he should research the available opportunities. He should first look at industries in general and narrow that down to specific jobs and companies, considering what is available in the areas he would consider working. He can look at trends in the labor market. He then needs to develop a plan for his career path. This might involve deciding on ways to get experience such as through an internship or volunteer position, and ways to learn such as through a student business organization. He should create a time frame for his plan. He might want to add flexibility to his plan, deciding what to do if the first plan doesn't work out. Finally, he should implement his plan by creating his resume, applying for jobs, practicing interviewing, and making a cover letter.

## Things for prospective employees to consider when creating career plans

There are many factors to consider when a prospective employee plans his (or her) career. First, he needs to consider his interests. Someone who likes to talk might want to venture into public relations, for instance. A person also has to consider what he is good at doing. Someone who is terrible at math would not want to go into accounting. In addition, an employee should decide what type of salary he desires as well as the working hours he is willing to work. He has to be realistic. He might have to put in long hours for a job that pays well. An employee should think about the environment he'd like to work in, as well as the opportunities available to him. He should not just think about now but also about the future and where he'd like his career to go. He should research potential opportunities, industries, and individual companies. He should map out his career and consider the timing.

## Sources of information about potential places of employment

There are a wide variety of sources where an individual can learn about potential places of employment. Career centers at schools provide a great resource. They help students connect with businesses that are hiring. Sometimes they set up interviews and/or offer meetings with potential employers. Employment agencies and recruiters can be useful. These specialize in connecting employees with employers. The Internet provides many ways to search for jobs. Individuals can search on one of the many job search websites such as Monster. These websites make it easy to upload resumes and apply. Job fairs provide another effective venue. Individuals can meet with potential employers. Many colleges and business schools offer these. Individuals can also look at classified advertisements in the newspapers or in trade publications. Personal networking is a very effective way as well. Individuals can "ask around" to people they know to see if they can connect with a potential employer.

## Gaining job skills and experience

A prospective employee can gain job skills and experience in many different ways, which can provide a valuable advantage when searching for a job. An internship is an excellent way to gain experience. A person can learn about a job as he (or she) works. Also, some jobs offer employment opportunities to their former interns. Job shadowing is another great way to attain experience. A person will follow and learn from a regular employee. An apprenticeship is another way to learn job skills. Individuals learn from someone who is skilled at the job and will typically get to practice it. Some people might get a part-time job in which they can get applicable experience. Volunteering is another way to gain experience. This can be especially useful in a field in which it is difficult to get a paying job with no experience at all. It is typically far easier to get volunteer work. Another choice is a school-to-work program, where students train for the jobs as they transition from an educational environment to a work one.

# Resume

A resume may be the first thing a potential employer sees, thus it is vital for it to be professional and comprehensive. First, a resume should contain all pertinent contact information including name, phone number, address, email, and website. It should contain an objective such as the type of position for which the employee is searching. It should contain information about an individual's education, including areas of study. If the GPA is impressive, it can be placed there. The resume should also list experience, especially the recent experience and that specifically related to the desired job. It should include pertinent information, such as dates of work, responsibilities, and accomplishments. It should list the individual's skills as well as accomplishments. A potential employee can list his (or her) activities and any awards or honors he received. Resumes should be thorough and contain information to validate claims. An impressive sales number is more powerful than simply saying the candidate is a good salesperson. All of the information should be pertinent and the document shouldn't be too long. It should be edited carefully so there are no errors.

## Strong cover letter

A strong cover letter can make all the difference in attaining a job. It is best to create a customized cover letter for each job; companies will appreciate the effort. It is important to address the letter to a specific person instead of "To Whom It May Concern." Potential employees should do research to find the correct recipient. Next, the letter should focus on how the employee can help the company and the skills, abilities, and experience that proves this. It should show impressive and substantiated information. For instance, someone who is hoping for a sales job may give impressive sales numbers from a previous job. A person should tailor this information to the details of the company and position. The cover letter should explain how the candidate meets the qualifications. It should not be just a generic letter. It should contain all pertinent information, including full contact information. It should be succinct and not too long—generally no more than one page—because employers are not going to spend a long time reading them. It should be professionally written and free of grammatical errors.

## Filling out strong job applications

A job application is one of the first documents a potential employer will see. When filling it out, a potential employee should use a black or blue pen or type it. An erasable pen can be useful. If printed, it should be extremely neat and large enough to be read. It is important to follow all directions on the job application. Everything should be filled out thoroughly, and there shouldn't be any blanks. If something doesn't apply, that should be indicated with "N/A" or a similar comment. Potential employees should explain any obvious issues such as if there was a long break between jobs. They should accentuate extremely pertinent information such as useful skills or statistics that highlight an advantage. Individuals should create a personal fact sheet they can bring with them to ensure all the information is accurate. They should check it over for accuracy and typographical errors.

## Interviewing for a job

An important step in preparing for a job interview is to practice interviewing. He (or she) should consider the most commonly asked questions and formulate and practice answers, preferably in front of someone who can evaluate him. He should research the company so he shows initiative and understanding of the company. He should prepare a resume, portfolio, business cards and other professional materials. A candidate should show up early to an interview, wearing professional clothing. He should be friendly and enthusiastic. He should show good body language, maintain eye contact, sit up straight, and not fidget. He should listen to the interviewers and answer the questions fully, putting the best light on his traits and highlighting how he can help the company. He should give valid data to support his points when possible. After the interview, he should follow up with a thank you card.

## CTSO

Career and technical student organizations (CTSO) are organizations dedicated to helping students learn and prepare for careers. There are many CTSOs dedicated to business students. Many offer local, regional, and/or national meetings and conferences where business students come together to network and to learn about trends in the business world. They help prepare students for careers and will sometimes offer mentoring and other opportunities. Many of the business CTSOs also offer competitions where students can compete in business-related events. These provide prizes and help students learn about business. They also look good on a resume. Students in these organizations also benefit from the knowledge and experience of the faculty advisors. Some of the organizations offer scholarships as well. They can be a great way for students to learn about business and the ways to embark on a business career.

### Benefits

Business students can learn about business careers and business in general through career and technical student organizations. It can be a great way to get pertinent experience. A CTSO also offers networking opportunities. Students mingle with those in the business world, which may help them gain an internship, a job, or other benefits that could lead to employment. A CTSO looks good on a resume because it shows initiative. In addition, many CTSOs offer competitive events. Doing well in these also looks good and exposes the student to more people in the business world. Some of them provide opportunities to be mentored. They can also be a resource when a business student is looking for a job. Students can meet other students, share information, and create relationships that may be useful in the future.

### Roles of faculty advisors

Faculty advisors provide information and guidance to business students in student organizations. They may provide information about business in general. Many of the organizations have competitions, and they help the students study and prepare for the competitions. They also help the students with their career goals and aspirations and help facilitate the meetings. Many faculty advisors will accompany the groups when attending local, regional, or national conferences. They provide information about the groups and help the students make the most of their membership. They might introduce the students to others in the business world and help with networking. In addition, many advisors will mentor business students. They provide a valuable function to the students.

## NBEA

The National Business Education Association (NBEA) is a professional organization for those involved in business education. It works to help members grow professionally and develop their skills in business education. It offers numerous publications; an informative national convention; networking opportunities at the local, regional and national levels; advocacy in legislative issues; opportunities to develop professionally; and information regarding international business. It offers numerous webinars to provide information and allows members to interact both in person and online in places such as Facebook, Twitter, and NBEAconnect. It also offers awards and scholarships. Meetings and conferences offer numerous workshops, educational sessions, and exhibitors.

## DECA

DECA started in 1946 with the goal of helping high school and college students prepare for business jobs in the fields of management, marketing, finance, and hospitality. With over 200,000 members, it provides a number of opportunities for those interested in the business field. One opportunity is to participate in numerous competitions. Students can learn about business and show off their skills, as well as gain something useful for their resumes. Another opportunity is to learn from one of over 5,000 advisors. Students get the chance to attend conferences and network. DECA also offers leadership conferences and career development conferences, which provide workshops and other opportunities to help students embark on their business careers.

## FBLA

The Future Business Leaders of America (FBLA) boasts over 200,000 members, making it the largest career organization for business students. It aspires to ready students for business and related jobs. It offers competitions, in which students can show off their business knowledge. It also offers informative literature, including *Tomorrow's Business Leader.* Conferences and seminars help students work on their leadership skills through workshops and exhibits. They can learn about current trends and ways to make their career goals come true. They can learn from each other and advisors, networking with those already in the business field. It has both local conferences and a national conference. It also offers leadership events and other special events for general members, as well as officers of the local chapters.

## BPA

With 43,000 members, the Business Professionals of America (BPA) is one of the largest career and technical student organizations for students interested in management, information technology, office administration, and similar careers. It seeks to prepare students for these careers through conferences, competitive events, and other resources, allowing students to hone their leadership, technological, citizenship, and academic skills. Conferences are organized at local, state, and national levels and offer the Workplace Skills Assessment Program (WSAP), which has 72 events in which students can learn and compete. It also offers scholarships, opportunities for officer positions, and a national Leadership Academy. It also allows for networking, both at a local and national level, and students can also learn from advisors. There are many advantages for students to join the BPA.

### Area chambers of commerce

Area chambers of commerce are organizations that allow local businesses to band together to work for the benefit of the business community as a whole. They range greatly in size, which is largely dependent on how large an area they represent. Businessmen can network and find ways to work with each other to benefit their businesses. Sometimes they work together to get favorable regulation or laws passed, although they do not have the ability to pass laws themselves. They may work with politicians to get initiatives that will benefit business. They may be non-profit, or the money may be provided by the government. They will generally have an executive council or a board of directors, as well as a CEO or similar individual to lead. It is advantageous for a business to join.

## Benefits of belonging to professional organizations

Many organizations offer workshops where teachers can learn about the latest trends in the business world. This can help them professionally, as well as give them information to disseminate to their students. In addition, business organizations provide opportunities to network at local, regional, and national conferences, as well as during meetings. Networking in the business world can be very positive and may help the business teacher move to a better position. Membership in a professional organization is also a good thing to have on a resume. It can look very prestigious. Many business education professional organizations also work to promote the interests of business education professionals, thus members can enjoy the benefits that come from these efforts. Many teachers may also enjoy interacting with others in the same field and with sharing and receiving information.  It is very worthwhile for business education teachers to join professional organizations.

# Practice Test

## Practice Questions

1. A command economy is characterized by:
   a. A laissez-faire approach by the government
   b. A moderate amount of government intervention in the economy
   c. Businesses commanding all aspects of the economy
   d. The government controlling prices and production

2. Which of the following is not a responsibility of the Securities and Exchange Commission (SEC)?
   a. Regulating securities
   b. Investigating insider trading
   c. Setting interest rates
   d. Processing applications for initial public offerings (IPOs)

3. In marketing, the demand for a product is directly influenced by:
   a. Customers' desire for a product
   b. Customers' ability to obtain a product
   c. Availability of a product
   d. Both A and B

4. The Sarbanes-Oxley Act of 2002:
   a. Vastly reduced the financial reporting obligations that corporations face
   b. Deregulated public utilities
   c. Was intended to fight corporate and accounting fraud
   d. Reduced tariffs on trade among North American countries

5. An employee earns $2,000.00 per month in gross pay, but pays $104.36 for health insurance, 9% in federal taxes, 3% for state taxes, and 2% for local taxes. What is the employee's net pay?
   a. $2,000.00
   b. $1,615.64
   c. $1,820.00
   d. $1,720.00

6. A market in which product availability exceeds demand is called a:
   a. Free market
   b. Seller's market
   c. Buyer's market
   d. Black market

7. Which of the following is not a part of Maslow's hierarchy of needs?
   a. Self-actualization
   b. Esteem
   c. Safety
   d. Supply and demand

8. Which of the following countries is not part of NAFTA?
    a. Mexico
    b. United States
    c. Canada
    d. China

9. A consumer's credit score is directly influenced by which of the following factors?
    a. Debt repayment history
    b. Employment history over the last five years
    c. Marital status
    d. Income level

10. Upon which organization does the international community primarily rely to deal with claims of unfair protectionism by one country against another?
    a. North Atlantic Treaty Organization (NATO)
    b. World Trade Organization (WTO)
    c. Organization of Petroleum Exporting Countries (OPEC)
    d. International Red Cross (IRC)

11. A homeowner is attempting to choose between several mortgage loans for a $200,000 home. Which of the following would have the lowest monthly payment?
    a. A 30-year fixed rate mortgage at 6%
    b. A 15-year fixed rate mortgage at 7%
    c. A 30-year fixed rate mortgage at 12%
    d. A 15-year fixed rate mortgage at 12%

12. The biggest factor that leads American companies to manufacture their products overseas in developing countries like China and India is:
    a. Higher quality of craftsmanship
    b. Lower labor costs
    c. Decreased transportation costs
    d. Effective legal systems

13. Which of the following correctly summarizes the accounting equation for a sole proprietorship?
    a. Assets = Liabilities + Owners' equity
    b. Liabilities = Assets + Owners' equity
    c. Owner's equity = Assets + Liabilities
    d. Revenue = Assets – Liabilities

14. In order to present a business plan to a group of potential investors, a businessperson would most likely use which software?
    a. Powerpoint
    b. Quickbooks
    c. Peoplesoft
    d. Excel

15. In order to start an online business, and individual would need all but which of the following:
    a. A business model
    b. A website
    c. An email address
    d. A fax machine

16. Which of the following types of assets would not be subject to depreciation?
    a. Heavy equipment
    b. Computers
    c. Real estate
    d. Company vehicles

17. When itemizing deductions on a federal tax return, an individual taxpayer may be able to deduct all but which of the following?
    a. Interest paid on a mortgage
    b. Charitable donations
    c. Losses from theft
    d. Groceries

18. Which of the following terms best describes a situation where an individual enters into an agreement with a company to use the company's business model within a given territory, usually in exchange for a fee?
    a. Sole proprietorship
    b. Limited liability corporation
    c. Franchise
    d. Incorporation

19. The par value of a bond is the:
    a. Average interest rate paid by a given type of bond over subsequent issues
    b. Amount of time until the bond matures
    c. Amount paid when the bond matures
    d. Amount of interest that the bond pays

20. Which of the following best describes Congress' purpose in setting up Freddie Mac in 1970?
    a. Expanding opportunities for home ownership
    b. Deregulating the credit market
    c. Improving regulation of the Internet
    d. Creating a place for small businesses to get loans

21. Which of the following countries would be considered an emerging market?
    a. Japan
    b. India
    c. Britain
    d. Canada

22. If the exchange rate between the Euro (€) and the U.S. dollar ($) is $2.5 to € 1, how many dollars would it take to purchase a plane ticket that costs € 1580.00?
  a. $39,500.00
  b. $3,950.00
  c. $395.00
  d. $632.00

23. If the U.S. Federal Reserve concludes that there is a significant risk of inflation, it will most likely:
  a. Raise interest rates
  b. Lower interest rates
  c. Keep interest rates the same
  d. Decrease bond yields

24. A combination of slow economic growth and high inflation is called:
  a. Inflationary pressure
  b. Deflation
  c. Stagflation
  d. Disinflation

25. A shareholder owns 200 shares of stock XYZ at $58 each. If there is a 2-1 stock split, how many shares will that shareholder have, and what will the new share price be?
  a. 100 shares at $116 per share
  b. 200 shares at $116 per share
  c. 400 shares at $29 per share
  d. 400 shares at $58 per share

26. Which of the following is not true of stock dividends?
  a. They are usually taxable
  b. They are offered voluntarily by companies in order to make their stock more attractive
  c. Their amount and frequency are determined directly by shareholders at large
  d. They may be discontinued or reduced at any time

27. If a stock has a high P/E ratio, this means that:
  a. The stock's price is low considering the value of the company's earnings
  b. The stock pays a high dividend based on its earnings per share
  c. The stock's price is high considering the value of its earnings per share
  d. The company's earnings per share are high

28. An individual who is about to retire and wants to earn interest without risking his or her principal would most likely be advised to invest in:
  a. Value stocks
  b. An index fund
  c. A mutual fund
  d. U.S. Treasury bonds

29. A company that is included in the Dow Jones Industrial Average most likely to be:
    a. A well-known corporation with a large market capitalization
    b. A foreign company
    c. A start-up that was recently listed on the stock exchange
    d. A small- to mid-sized technology company

Table 1

|  | Investor A | Investor B | Investor C | Investor D |
|---|---|---|---|---|
| Stocks | 20% | 85% | 70% | 50% |
| Bonds | 70% | 10% | 20% | 50% |
| Cash | 10% | 5% | 10% | 0% |

30. Which of the investors in Table 1 has the portfolio that is exposed to the greatest amount of risk?
    a. Investor A
    b. Investor B
    c. Investor C
    d. Investor D

31. Refer again to Table 1. If Investor D's stocks have an average return of 8.8% during the year, and Investor D's bonds have an average return of 5.2%, what is the average overall return on Investor D's portfolio?
    a. 14%
    b. 7%
    c. 5.6%
    d. Cannot be determined

32. If one is planning to start a small business, which should one do first?
    a. Obtain a business loan
    b. Find a partner
    c. Assess one's personal financial situation
    d. Choose a location for one's business

33. Frank is 33 years old and married, with 2 children. He has $40,000 in his retirement account, which is earning an average of 5% annually, and $10,000 in his personal savings account, which is earning 2% annually. He is current with his mortgage, and has $50,000 left to pay at a rate of 6%. Frank also has $30,000 in credit card debt with an average rate of 13%. If Frank wants to increase his chances of retiring comfortably, what would the best way be for him to spend a Christmas bonus of $10,000?
    a. Put it in his retirement account
    b. Put it in his savings account
    c. Use half to pay down his mortgage and save the other half
    d. Use all of it to pay down his credit card debt

34. If a country is a net exporter, this means that:
    a. The value of the goods that it imports exceeds the value of the goods that it exports
    b. The value of the goods that it exports exceeds the value of the goods that it imports
    c. It exports consumer products
    d. It has high tariffs

35. If a government implements an import tariff on consumer electronics, what is it most likely trying to accomplish?
   a. It is trying to protect its domestic consumer electronics industry from competition
   b. It is trying to decrease the cost of imported consumer electronics
   c. It is trying to discourage domestic companies from producing consumer electronics
   d. It is trying to increase competition and lower prices in the consumer electronics industry

36. If a potential business owner projects that she will need to invest $100,000 in equipment to start a dry cleaning business, and the business' monthly expenses on rent, insurance, labor costs, and other incidentals are $5,000, how many months will it take for her to earn back her initial investment if the average monthly gross revenue is $8,000?
   a. Less than 9 months
   b. Less than 20 months
   c. Less than 34 months
   d. None of the above

Table 2

|  | Sticker price of the car | Down payment | Monthly payment | Term of loan |
|---|---|---|---|---|
| Option A | $8,000 | $0 | $330 | 36 months |
| Option B | $8,000 | $3,000 | $160 | 60 months |
| Option C | $15,000 | $0 | $250 | 60 months |
| Option D | $15,000 | $5,000 | $400 | 36 months |

37. Refer to Table 2 above. A family wants to buy a new car, and is trying to decide between four different car and car loan options. Which of the loans would require them to pay the least amount of money overall, including the down payment and the monthly payments?
   a. Option A
   b. Option B
   c. Option C
   d. Option D

38. Which of the four options listed in Table 2 would require the family to pay the least amount of interest, total?
   a. Option A
   b. Option B
   c. Option C
   d. Option D

39. Which of the options listed in Table 2 would require the family to pay the highest amount of interest, total?
   a. Option A
   b. Option B
   c. Option C
   d. Option D

Table 3

| | Cost | Franchise fee | Average gross monthly revenue | Average monthly expenses |
|---|---|---|---|---|
| Business A | $500,000 | 5% of gross revenue | $20,000 | $15,000 |
| Business B | $440,000 | 4% of gross revenue | $16,000 | $10,000 |
| Business C | $320,000 | None | $10,000 | $5,000 |
| Business D | $175,000 | None | $8,000 | $5,000 |

40. Refer to Table 3. Sarah has up to $550,000 to invest, and is trying to decide which of four catering businesses she wants to purchase. Which of the options below correctly lists the businesses in order of average monthly profit from largest to smallest when the franchise fee is taken into consideration?
    a. A, B, C, D
    b. C, D, A, B
    c. B, C, A, D
    d. C, B, A, D

41. If Sarah wanted to get her initial investment back as quickly as possible, which of the following options would you advise her to choose, based upon the information in Table 3?
    a. Business A
    b. Business B
    c. Business C
    d. Business D

42. A consumer's credit score may be factor in all but which of the following transactions?
    a. Buying a car
    b. Buying a home
    c. Getting a personal loan
    d. Opening a bank account

43. Comprehensive car insurance typically covers:
    a. Damage the insured does to the property of others while driving the insured vehicle
    b. Medical expenses others incur as a result of a collision with the insured vehicle
    c. Damage done to the insured's vehicle by a vandal
    d. All of the above

44. Which of the following is not typically cited as a potential cause of oil price increases?
    a. Price increases for consumer goods and services in the U.S.
    b. Increased global demand for oil
    c. Speculation in the oil market
    d. Insufficient refinery capacity

45. Nations whose economies rely primarily of the export of non-oil commodities like rubber or copper are:
    a. Typically located in Northern and Western Europe
    b. Often referred to as "developing countries" or "emerging markets"
    c. Known for their world class education systems
    d. Usually among the wealthiest countries in the world

46. A company considering manufacturing a product in several different emerging markets will most likely consider which of the following factors in choosing between them?
    a. Likelihood of political instability
    b. Labor costs and regulations
    c. Cost of shipping goods from that country to the destination country
    d. All of the above

47. Adam Smith is best known for:
    a. Founding the doctrine of mercantilism
    b. Supporting the spread of communism
    c. Arguing for free market economics
    d. Arguing that the government should redistribute income

48. According to standard economic theories, countries that have a comparative advantage in the production of cotton should:
    a. Export another product, and import cotton
    b. Export cotton, and import other products
    c. Implement tariffs to protect their domestic cotton industry
    d. Work hard to reduce their comparative advantage and diversify their economy

49. An advantage of protectionism for countries that implement it is that it:
    a. Improves the country's global competitiveness
    b. Ensures that domestic jobs will be retained in the short term
    c. Encourages economic growth
    d. Prevents corruption

50. GDP measures a country's:
    a. Employment level
    b. Education level
    c. Total economic output
    d. Wage levels

51. A human resources manager is likely to be responsible for all but which of the following:
    a. Sales
    b. Payroll
    c. Hiring
    d. Training

52. The main function of a human resources department is to:
    a. Meet the company's recruiting goals
    b. Maximize employee productivity while minimizing pay
    c. Facilitate communication between the employer and the employees
    d. Prevent lawsuits

53. Which of the following questions would it be illegal to ask a job candidate at a pre-employment interview?
   a. Have you ever requested workers' compensation benefits?
   b. Do you have any disabilities that would interfere with your ability to perform this job?
   c. Both A and B
   d. Neither A nor B

54. Technological aids can be used to directly fulfill all but which of the following human resources functions:
   a. Soliciting resumes for open positions
   b. Assessing a new employee's job readiness
   c. Communicating information about employee benefits
   d. Resolving disputes between employees and management

55. A new manager with ABC Industries has noticed that many of his employees are chronically late to work. To remedy the problem, the manager decides to implement a bonus system that will financially reward employees who are on time to work for ten consecutive days. According to B.F. Skinner's Operant Conditioning theory, what type of behavior modification approach is the manager using?
   a. Extinction
   b. Punishment
   c. Negative reinforcement
   d. Positive reinforcement

Table 4

| Management Approach | Characteristic |
| --- | --- |
| 1. Classical Theory | A. Productivity can be improved through the application of mathematical models |
| 2. Behavioral Theory | B. Understanding the worker's perspective is key to successful management |
| 3. Management Science Approach | C. There is no single "correct" theory; instead, managers should apply the theory that is most sensible in a given situation |
| 4. Contingency Approach | D. Productivity can be maximized by presenting the right combination of incentives, and correctly designing jobs |

56. Refer to Table 4, and correctly match each Management Approach in the right column with the characteristic in the left column that best describes it.
   a. 1-D, 2-B, 3-A, 4-C
   b. 1-A, 2-C, 3-B, 4-D
   c. 1-A, 2-C, 3-D, 4-B
   d. 1-D, 2-A, 3-B, 4-C

57. A successful manager will be able to effectively delegate:
    a. Responsibility
    b. Accountability
    c. Authority
    d. Ability

58. According to Fayol's Administrative Theory of Management, which of the following is a correct
    list of the five essential functions of management?
    a. Controlling, composing, planning, organizing, implementing
    b. Containing, controlling, implementing, planning, organizing
    c. Composing, coordinating, controlling, planning, organizing
    d. Controlling, commanding, coordinating, planning, organizing

59. According to the National Environmental Policy Act of 1967, a business is required to prepare
an environmental impact statement (EIS) when it:
    a. Hires a new worker
    b. Makes a charitable contribution
    c. Develops a new marketing initiative
    d. Builds a new factory

60. A manufacturing company implements anti-pollution measures as outlined by applicable
legislation, but opts not to adopt any additional anti-pollution measures. This company has most
likely adopted which of the following approaches to business-society relations?
    a. Social Responsiveness Approach
    b. Social Responsibility Approach
    c. Social Obligation Approach
    d. Cost-benefit Approach

61. Which of the following constitutes a binding contract?
    a. An agreement signed and dated by one party and one witness
    b. An agreement signed and dated by both parties
    c. An agreement signed by both parties and witnessed by a third party
    d. An agreement signed and dated by both parties and a witness

62. Corporation X, the largest oil refiner in the U.S., wants to purchase Corporation Y, the only other
oil refiner in the U.S. This situation may be of concern to the government because:
    a. It may violate environmental laws
    b. It may constitute a violation of antitrust laws
    c. It could violate labor laws by reducing employees' choice of employers
    d. It could constitute a pyramid scheme

63. The Equal Employment Opportunity Commission (EEOC) is responsible for enforcing all but
which of the following laws?
    a. Civil Rights Act of 1964
    b. Equal Pay Act
    c. Environmental Protection Act
    d. Americans with Disabilities Act ·

64. Anna is interested in purchasing a computer for her small landscaping business. She wants to be able to compose simple fliers and advertising materials, communicate with clients via email, and order supplies online. Which of the following lists best describes the hardware and software components that Anna's computer should have?
    a. Internet connection, Quickbooks, and at least 10 GB of memory
    b. Word processing software, Quickbooks, and an Internet connection
    c. Word processing software, an Internet connection, and 1-5 GB of memory
    d. Quickbooks, an Internet connection, and 1-5 GB of memory

65. Microsoft Excel would most likely be used for which of the following tasks?
    a. Developing a strategic plan
    b. Filing invoices
    c. Creating a sales presentation
    d. Analyzing numerical sales data

66. Which of the following steps might a company take in order to prevent unauthorized individuals from accessing confidential data?
    a. Requiring a username and password to access its computer system
    b. Constructing a firewall to protect its computer system
    c. Both A and B
    d. Neither A nor B

67. In order to facilitate communication between employees within a company, the company is considering providing all employees with unlimited access to a file that contains employee names, work phone numbers and addresses, work email addresses, birthdates, and social security numbers. What confidentiality issues would this new policy raise?
    a. None, the value of improved communication between employees would outweigh any confidentiality issues
    b. Many employees may object to their social security numbers and birthdays being shared with others; the company should publish the birthdays anyway, but withhold the social security numbers
    c. Many employees may object to their social security numbers and birthdays being shared with others; the company should withhold both of these
    d. Releasing of any of this information is a violation of employees' privacy

68. A business education teacher has allotted one class period to help students identify potential career options. Which of the following activities would be most appropriate given these circumstances?
    a. Having students complete an internship
    b. Having each student deliver a five-minute presentation describing their parents' jobs
    c. Administering a test that advises students about what careers might fit their interests and talents
    d. Asking students to write an essay describing their "dream job"

69. Which of the following business careers could a teacher safely recommend for a student who would not enjoy working with the public on a regular basis?
    a. Financial advisor
    b. Insurance salesperson
    c. Real estate agent
    d. None of the above

70. Choose the list below that best describes the most important contents of a resume:
    a. Salary requirements, relevant work experience, educational attainment, objective
    b. Contact information, grade point average, relevant work experience, objective
    c. References, objective, educational attainment, salary requirements
    d. Contact information, objective, educational attainment, relevant work experience

71. At a meeting with shareholders, an executive would be most likely to use which of the following visual aids to present a report on monthly stock gains and losses over a one-year period?
    a. Bar chart
    b. Pie chart
    c. Line graph
    d. Scatterplot

72. When manually proofreading a business document for a colleague, which of the following answers describes the correct way one would indicate that a section of text should be removed?
    a. An X should be drawn through the text
    b. A caret should be drawn at the beginning and end of the text
    c. A diagonal line should be drawn through the text from bottom left to top right
    d. A horizontal line should be drawn through the text with a loop at the right end of the line

73. When researching a presentation about a national shipping business, the most detailed and comprehensive source of information about the top management of the company and its competitors would most likely be:
    a. Microfilm records from local newspapers
    b. Hoovers.com
    c. LexisNexis.com
    d. The catalogue at your local library

74. Which of the following lists contains only types of computer software?
    a. Internet, Microsoft Office, Quicken
    b. Motherboard, Quicken, Excel
    c. Quicken, Peoplesoft, Microsoft Office
    d. Monitor, Mouse, Keyboard

75. Search engine optimization (SEO) is the process of:
    a. Designing a search engine to operate as efficiently as possible
    b. Designing a website to maximize its placement in search engine results for particular keywords, thus increasing traffic to the site
    c. Improving the visual aesthetic of a search engine
    d. Making a search engine more user-friendly

76. On the Internet, links are used in all but which of the following ways?
    a. They direct Internet users to other websites that have additional relevant information
    b. They are used for marketing purposes, to entice Internet users to navigate away from one website to view another one
    c. They allow Internet users to open additional windows that explain a webpage's content or provide technical assistance
    d. They allow computer users to open software programs on their PC

77. When designing a website for an online business, the web developer would include a site map in order to:
    a. Give website users directions to the business
    b. Provide website users with a list of links to all of the pages on the website
    c. Convince website users that it is safe to purchase products from the website
    d. Help website users decide which products to buy from the website

78. Better Business Bureau certification is useful for businesses that engage in e-commerce because it:
    a. Protects them from legal action by defrauded consumers
    b. Exempts them from paying state taxes
    c. Proves that they are certified by the government
    d. Reassures customers that the company is reliable

79. Businesses can increase the security of confidential customer information by:
    a. Destroying paper records of credit card information
    b. Conducting employee background checks
    c. Installing a firewall and virus protection software for computer systems
    d. All of the above

80. A high school student expresses interest in starting her own auto repair business after graduating from high school. She could best prepare for such a career by:
    a. Getting a college degree in finance and then completing an MBA program
    b. Taking small business finance, law, and accounting courses
    c. Getting an internship or part time job at an auto-repair shop
    d. B and C only

81. A business education teacher wants to evaluate her program in terms of how well graduates are prepared for the workforce. Which of the following strategies would be most likely to provide the best data to answer this question?
    a. Setting up an advisory committee of local employers to gather feedback on graduates' performance in the workplace
    b. Asking students to complete internships with local employers
    c. Conducting a survey of recent graduates to see if they were able to find jobs with local employers
    d. Asking the business professors at a local community college to provide feedback

82. Which of the following activities that are conducted by high school student leadership organizations would be the most effective tool for teaching business skills?
    a. Raising money by selling concessions at athletic events
    b. Performing community service by painting a local elementary school
    c. Holding an awards ceremony to honor scholarship winners
    d. Tutoring middle school students in math and reading

83. A business education teacher is asked to serve as an advisor to the local chapter of a student leadership organization. The teacher's primary responsibility as an advisor is most likely to:
    a. Ensure that students follow established procedures for conducting meetings
    b. Ensure the health and safety of student participants in the organization
    c. Design and implement activities for the group
    d. Collect and account for dues and fundraising proceeds

84. Which of the following activities provides the best example of collaboration between business education teachers and teachers of other subject areas?
    a. Students in a business education class are asked to write cover letters and resumes
    b. Students in a business education class read case studies about research and development for new products
    c. A business education teacher and a math teacher coordinate their lesson plans so that the concepts taught in math class are subsequently applied to real situations in the business class
    d. Students in a business class learn to balance checkbooks

85. Which of the following activities would most effectively and comprehensively assess students' mastery of learning objectives for a unit about small business?
    a. Asking students to create and market a new invention
    b. Asking students to design and implement a community service project
    c. Requiring students to complete an internship or externship
    d. Having students write and present a business plan

86. A business education teacher wants students to complete an activity that teaches them skills that are necessary for working in a culturally diverse environment. Which of the following activities would fulfill this goal?
    a. Collaborating with the social studies teacher to teach students about work customs in other cultures
    b. Asking students to read and discuss written accounts of minorities' experiences in the workplace
    c. Teaching students about laws and regulations that protect people from diverse ethnic and cultural backgrounds
    d. All of the above

Table 5

| Name of Business | Credit Rating |
|---|---|
| Business A | BBB |
| Business B | BB |
| Business C | AA |
| Business D | AAA |

87. Based on the information in Table 5, which of the following lists correctly orders the businesses from least to most risky for investors?
    a. Business B, Business A, Business C, Business D
    b. Business A, Business B, Business D, Business C
    c. Business D, Business C, Business A, Business B
    d. Business C, Business D, Business B, Business A

Table 6

| Time card: Scott Smith | | |
|---|---|---|
| Date | Clock in | Clock out |
| 11/01 | 11:00 AM | 3:00 PM |
| 11/02 | 8:00 AM | 12:00 PM |
| 11/03 | 8:00 AM | 12:00 PM |
| 11/05 | 11:00 AM | 3:00 PM |
| 11/07 | 8:00 AM | 12:00 PM |

88. If part time employee Scott Smith, whose time card is shown in Table 6, is paid $10.00 per hour on weekdays (Monday-Friday), and $11.00 per hour on weekends, and November 1st is a Monday, how much should he be paid for the week of November 1st through November 7th?
    a. $160.00
    b. $200.00
    c. $204.00
    d. $240.00

89. Only full time employees of Scott Smith's company, whose time card is shown in Table 6, have health insurance and 401k benefits deducted from their paychecks. Based on the number of hours Smith worked from November 1st through November 7th, which of the following is a correct list of his payroll deductions if he is a W-4 employee?
    a. 401k and health insurance
    b. Social security and Medicare
    c. Social security, Medicare, and income taxes
    d. None of the above

90. The company that Scott Smith works for provides full time employees with a 100% 401k match after one year on the job if they contribute 4% of their paycheck. If Scott becomes a full time employee after a year, makes $2,000 per paycheck, and contributes 4% to his 401k each pay period, how much would the company have to contribute to his 401k during each pay period?
    a. $160
    b. $80
    c. $40
    d. Cannot be determined

91. Accounts receivable are:
    a. Fixed assets
    b. Fixed liabilities
    c. Current assets
    d. Current liabilities

92. Owners' equity is comprised of:
    a. The personal net worth of the owners plus the amount of their initial investment in the business
    b. The amount of the owners' initial investment in the business
    c. The owners' unclaimed profits from the business' operation
    d. Both B and C

93. Which of the following are not protected by copyright law?
     a. Architectural drawings
     b. Scripts for plays
     c. Advertising slogans
     d. Books of poetry

94. A phrase that is associated with a particular product would be protected by which of the following?
     a. Trademark law
     b. Patent law
     c. Copyright law
     d. Both A and C

95. Which of the following is true of a corporation?
     a. It is always owned by shareholders
     b. Its shareholders are personally liable if it fails
     c. Its board of directors is personally liable if it fails
     d. It cannot sue another entity or be sued

96. Which of the following would be a violation of the Occupational Safety and Health Act (OSHA)?
     a. An employee becoming injured while commuting to work
     b. An employee becoming injured because an employer did not provide equipment in good working order
     c. An employer requiring employees to work with toxic chemicals
     d. An employer failing to accompany an OSHA compliance officer on an inspection

97. The following are each sentences from a job description. Select the sentence that clearly and correctly communicates its intended meaning.
     a. The employee, will have excellent oral communication skills.
     b. The employees oral communication skills will be excellent.
     c. The employee will communicate orally and in writing well.
     d. The employee will have excellent writing skills.

98. Which of the following is true of a Wide Area Network (WAN)?
     a. A WAN is equivalent to a LAN
     b. Businesses usually have their own WAN
     c. The Internet is an example of a WAN
     d. Businesses prefer WANs to LANs because their data transfer speed is higher

99. A business education teacher teaches two classes of 30 9th graders during a semester. At the end of the class, students are given identical tests of the course material. Students in Class 1, which was taught using a traditional lecture approach, scored an average of 73% on the test. Students in Class 2, which was taught using interactive exercises and computer-based simulations, scored an average of 82% on the test. What can be concluded from this experiment?
     a. The students in Class 2 are more intelligent than those in Class 1
     b. The teaching methods used for Class 2 are superior to those used for Class 1
     c. Nothing can be concluded from these results because one semester is not a long enough period of time to accurately measure learning
     d. Nothing can be concluded from these results because students' baseline performance on these tests was not measured before the experiment

*- 108 -*

100. Which of the following would violate federal child labor regulations?
   a. Hiring your own child to work in your small business if the child is under 14
   b. Employing someone under 14 as a newspaper carrier
   c. Employing someone under 18 in a job deemed hazardous
   d. Employing anyone under 18 as a babysitter

# Constructed Response

You have purchased a business that sells prescription eyeglasses. Sales have recently decreased, although demand for these products appears to be high, and competitors have maintained the same level of sales. The highest-selling product, which has been on the market for three years and is targeted to consumers ages 20 to 29, has experienced the most significant decrease in sales. Currently, all advertising is done via direct mail and radio broadcast. Customers often complain about the slow processing of orders. Frequently, items must be placed on back order because they are not in stock.

Using your knowledge of marketing strategies and inventory control, prepare a response in which you use the information above to propose strategies to:

- Improve advertising campaigns, especially those for products popular with younger audiences
- Achieve general customer satisfaction
- Increase overall sales and brand recognition

# Answers and Explanations

1. D: A command economy (also known as a planned economy) is characterized by the government controlling nearly all aspects of the economy, including prices and production. This type of economy is traditionally associated with Communist economies where prices, wages and production quotas are set by the government. A, B, and C are all incorrect because they imply some form of private sector autonomy.

2. C: The Securities and Exchange Commission (SEC) is responsible for regulating securities, investigating insider trading, and processing applications for initial public offerings (IPOs) of stock. However, the Federal Reserve is responsible for setting interest rates.

3. D: In marketing, the demand for a product is determined both by customers' desire for that product, coupled with their ability to obtain it if they want it. For example, even if customers want a product, demand for it may be decreased if it is illegal or prohibitively expensive. Answer C, availability of a given product, refers to supply, not demand.

4. C: The Sarbanes-Oxley Act of 2002 was intended to fight corporate and accounting fraud in the wake of several huge scandals that brought down major U.S corporations. This bill reformed the rules and regulations governing corporations' financial disclosures, and increased financial reporting obligations.

5. B: The employee's net pay, or total take-home pay after deductions, is $1,615.64. This is calculated by subtracting the employee's taxes (totaling 14%, or $280.00) and insurance ($104.36 ) from the gross pay of $2,000.00.

6. C: A market in which product availability is greater than product demand is called a buyer's market, because when supply (product availability) exceeds demand, the prices paid by buyers decrease. This decrease in prices benefits the buyer of a product and decreases the seller's profits.

7. D: Supply and demand is not a part of Maslow's hierarchy of needs. This hierarchy is part of Maslow's theory that once people satisfy basic needs like food, water, and physical security, they begin to pursue needs higher up the hierarchy, like social acceptance, self-esteem, and self-actualization.

8. D: China is not part of NAFTA. NAFTA refers to the North American Free Trade Agreement, which is an agreement to encourage trade between the U.S., Canada, and Mexico.

9. A: A consumer's credit score is directly influenced by the individual's payment history on car and home loans, credit cards, etc. While marital status, employment history, and income level may indirectly influence the credit score by affecting the consumer's ability to pay bills on time, only payment history itself is a direct factor in credit score calculations.

10. B: The primary organization upon which the international community relies to deal with claims of unfair protectionism by one country against another is the World Trade Organization (WTO). NATO is a military alliance among many North American and European countries, OPEC is an organization of oil-producing countries that regulates supply and prices, and the Red Cross is an international humanitarian organization.

11. A: A 30-year fixed rate mortgage at 6% would provide the lowest monthly payment on the $200,000 mortgage loan, because it has both the longest term (30 years) and the lowest interest rate (6%). This means that the consumer would be paying less interest on a yearly basis, and the total would be divided over the maximum number of monthly payments.

12. B: The biggest factor that leads American companies to manufacture their products in developing countries is lower labor cost. Labor costs in developing countries (countries with a comparatively low GDP per capita) are lower than in the U.S. because unemployment is higher and labor regulations are less stringent.

13. A: The accounting equation for a sole proprietorship is correctly stated as Assets = Liabilities + Owners' equity. In the accounting equation for a corporation, owners' equity is replaced by shareholders' equity.

14. A: In order to present a business plan to a group of potential investors, a businessperson would most likely use Powerpoint, which allows an individual to present text and pictures in a slide format using a PC. Quickbooks is used for accounting, Peoplesoft is used by human resources professionals, and Excel is used for storing and analyzing numerical and categorical data.

15. D: In order to start an online business, an individual would need an Internet connection, email, and a web domain, but a fax machine would not necessarily be required, since documents can be scanned and sent via email.

16. C: Real estate is not subject to depreciation. While real estate often appreciates (increases) in value, assets like vehicles and computer equipment inevitably depreciate (decline in value) due to normal wear and tear.

17. D: When itemizing deductions on a federal tax return, a taxpayer may be able to deduct all of the things listed here except for food costs. Mortgage interest, losses from theft and charitable donations are all tax-deductible under certain circumstances.

18. C: When an individual enters into an agreement with a company to use the company's business model within a given territory, this is called a franchise agreement. In most cases, the individual pays the company a franchise fee, usually a percentage of gross revenue, in order to use the company's business model.

19. C: The par value of a bond is the value of the bond when it is issued. The par value is typically the amount that the bond issuer pays the buyer when the bond matures, as well.

20. A: Expanding opportunities for home ownership was Congress' primary purpose in setting up Freddie Mac. This organization was charged with increasing the availability of money for home loans by pooling mortgages together to create mortgage-backed securities.

21. B: India is the only country listed here that would be considered an emerging market. Emerging markets exist only in countries that are in the process of rapidly industrializing. Countries like Britain, Japan, and Canada have slower-growing, mature economies that have long passed the emergent stage. As in the case of India, emerging markets are often the destination for outsourced jobs.

22. B: If the exchange rate between the Euro (€) and the U.S. dollar ($) is $2.5 to € 1, it would take $3,950.00 to purchase a plane ticket that costs € 1580.00. This is calculated by multiplying the number of dollars to one Euro (2.5) by the cost of the plane ticket in Euros (1580).

23. A: If the U.S. Federal Reserve concludes that there is a significant risk of inflation, it will most likely raise interest rates. By raising interest rates, a central bank like the Federal Reserve can increase the cost of borrowing money, thus slowing economic growth and the price inflation that results from increased demand.

24. C: A combination of slow economic growth and high inflation is called stagflation. This can occur when slow economic growth (little or none of the wage and job increases that create demand) is coupled with price increases caused by external factors like rising energy costs.

25. C: If a shareholder owns 200 shares of stock XYZ at $58 each and there is a 2-1 stock split, the shareholder would then own 400 shares at $29 per share. Companies split stock in order to decrease the price and stimulate trading. In a two for one split, the number of shares is doubled, but the price is halved.

26. C: Stock dividends are usually taxable, they may be discontinued or reduced at any time, and they are offered voluntarily by companies to make their stock more attractive. However, the amount and frequency of dividend payments are determined by the company's board of directors, not by shareholders at large.

27. C: If a stock has a high P/E ratio, this means that the stock's price is high considering the value of its earnings per share (EPS). The P/E ratio is calculated by dividing the share price by the company's EPS. The closer the result is to zero, the cheaper the stock is in relation to the amount of money the company is earning.

28. D: An individual who is about to retire and wants to earn interest without risking his or her principal would most likely be advised to invest in U.S. Treasury bonds. Value stocks, index funds, and mutual funds are all tied to the stock market, which is far more volatile and risky than U.S. Treasury bonds. (Some other bond investments, like junk bonds, can be quite risky). Since this investor is more concerned with protecting the principal than with earning high returns, an investment in bonds would best match his or her objective.

29. A: A company that is included in the Dow Jones Industrial Average most likely would be a well-known corporation with a large market capitalization. The Dow lists only thirty companies, most of which are household names.

30. B: Investor B is exposed to the greatest amount of risk, because 85% of the money in Investor B's portfolio is invested in stocks. Stocks are historically riskier than bonds or cash, so Investor B is more vulnerable than the other investors to large market fluctuations. However, this also means that Investor B has the largest potential to earn higher returns.

31. The correct answer is B, 7%. If stocks return 8.8% during the year, and bonds return 5.2%, then Investor D's overall return would be the average of both halves of the portfolio, since 50% was in bonds and 50% was in stocks. The overall return is equal to the weighted average of the returns from all investments, in this case the average of 8.8% and 5.2%.

32. C: If one is planning to start a small business, one's first step should be to assess one's personal financial situation in order to determine how much start-up capital one has, and how long one can afford to support oneself before one's business begins to turn a profit. Conducting these types of calculations will help one determine how large a loan one needs to request, and whether one needs a partner. Banks would also require this information before they issued a loan.

33. D: Frank could improve his chances for a comfortable retirement by using the $10,000 bonus to pay down his high interest credit card debt. Since the high interest rate on the credit card debt means that Frank is paying more in interest than he would be earning in either his savings account or his retirement account, paying down this debt will increase his ability to save over the long term. Since the credit card interest rate is higher than the mortgage interest rate, the credit card should be paid off first.

34. B: If a country is a net exporter, this means that the value of the goods that it exports exceeds the value of the goods that it imports. Net exporters have positive trade balances, meaning that the value of the goods that they sell to other countries exceeds the value of the goods that they buy from other countries.

35. A: If a government implements a tariff on imported consumer electronics, it is most likely trying to protect its domestic consumer electronics industry from foreign competition. By increasing tariffs, the government will increase the domestic prices for foreign-made consumer electronics, thus making domestically-produced products more attractive to consumers and reducing the overall level of competition in the industry.

36. C: If the business owner has invested $100,000 into the business, and makes an average monthly profit of $3,000 ($8,000 average gross revenue minus the $5,000 monthly costs of running the business), it will take approximately 33.3 months for her to make back her initial $100,000 investment.

37. A: If the family is looking for the lowest overall cost, Option A would total only $11,880 ($330 multiplied by 36 months). Option B would cost $12,600 overall, option C would cost $15,000, and option D would cost $19,400, including the down payment and monthly payments.

38. C: If the family wanted to ensure that they pay the lowest amount of interest possible, Option C would be the best choice. The total cost of the car, $15,000, divided by the number of payments (60) equals the monthly payment exactly, meaning that the family pays no interest at all for this option. Interest can be calculated by subtracting the car's sticker price from the total amount actually paid over the life of the loan.

39. B: Option B would require the family to pay the highest amount of interest total. Option B pays a total of $12,600 ($160 multiplied by 60 months plus $3000 in down payment) for an $8,000 vehicle, so $4,600 of that payment is interest. The others have lower interest payments.

40. C: Business B has the highest average monthly profit, at $5,360. This is calculated by adding the franchise fee to the total monthly expenditures, and subtracting this total from the average gross monthly revenue. Business C makes an average monthly profit of $5,000, Business A makes around $4,000 per month, and Business D makes just $3,000 per month.

41. D: If Sarah wanted to get her initial investment back as quickly as possible, she would be best advised to choose Business D, which would allow her to recoup her initial investment of $175,000

in just over 58 months. One can estimate how long it will take to recoup the initial investment for a business by dividing the cost of buying the business by the average monthly profit.

42. D: A consumer's credit score may be considered when a consumer buys a car or home if the transaction involves a loan, and it will also be considered if an individual applies for a personal loan. However, one's credit score is not considered when opening a bank account, because the account holder is depositing money rather than borrowing it.

43. C: Comprehensive insurance typically covers damage due to vandalism. Collision insurance typically covers damage done to other people's property while driving the insured vehicle, and the medical expenses of people in a collision with the insured vehicle.

44. A: Many economists argue that price increases for consumer goods and services in the U.S. increase as a result of oil price increases, but they are not typically cited as a potential cause of them.

45. B: Nations whose economies rely primarily on the export of non-oil commodities like rubber or copper are often referred to as "developing countries" or "emerging markets." Because of the instability of commodity prices, and these countries' often disproportionate reliance on commodity exports, developing countries are typically poorer and less able to provide social services than are countries that rely more heavily on manufacturing and service industries.

46. D: All of the above. Political instability could put the company's investment at risk, and the labor and shipping costs associated with a given country can be a decisive factor in investment decisions.

47. C: Adam Smith is best known for writing *The Wealth of Nations*, a treatise on free market economics in which he describes an "invisible hand" which guides the marketplace through individuals protecting their own self-interest. He argued that economic competition through a free market would be the best way to increase economic efficiency, productivity, and ultimately human happiness.

48. B: Economic theory states that countries with a comparative advantage in producing a particular product should produce and export that product, and use the proceeds to import the other products that they need from other countries.

49. B: An advantage of protectionism for countries that implement it is that it helps ensure that domestic jobs will be retained in the short term. By implementing protectionist measures that decrease the competitiveness of otherwise cheaper foreign goods, governments can protect the domestic industries that produce those goods and preserve the jobs of the people who work in them.

50. C: GDP (gross domestic product) measures a country's total economic output, including goods and services, over a given period of time. Usually, GDP is reported annually.

51. A: A human resources manager is likely to be responsible for hiring, training, and payroll, but not sales. Human resources managers are in charge of employer-employee relations, including any activity that involves recruiting and retaining valuable employees.

52. C: The main function of a human resources department is to facilitate communication between the employer and the employees. While human resources departments are primarily responsible to

the company's upper management, they are intended to provide a "neutral" conduit through which personnel policies can be devised and implemented, and through which employees can express and resolve concerns.

53. C: It would be illegal to ask either of the questions listed in answers A and B at a job interview. The Americans with Disabilities Act prohibits employers from attempting to ascertain a prospective employee's disability status prior to hiring the job candidate. Questions like, "Have you ever requested workers' compensation benefits," or, "Do you have any disabilities that would interfere with your ability to perform this job," would both fall into this category of illegal interview questions.

54. D: Technological aids such as email and computer software programs can be used to directly fulfill human resources functions like soliciting resumes for open positions, assessing a new employee's job readiness, or communicating information about employee benefits. However, a complicated situation such as an employee-employer dispute requires listening and negotiation skills and judgment that cannot be replaced by a computer.

55. D: The manager is using positive reinforcement. According to Skinner's theory, undesirable behavior such as tardiness can be dealt with using positive reinforcement, negative reinforcement, punishment, or extinction (discontinuing an existing practice that encourages or rewards that behavior).

56. A: The Classical Theory of management argues that productivity can be maximized by presenting the right combination of incentives, and correctly designing jobs. The Behavioral Theory emphasizes that understanding the worker's perspective is key to successful management, and the Management Science approach asserts that productivity can be improved through the application of mathematical models. More recently, proponents of the Contingency Approach have argued that there is no single "correct" theory; instead, managers should apply the theory that is most sensible in a given situation.

57. C: A successful manager will be able to effectively delegate authority. As a leader, the manager always retains accountability for results and ultimate responsibility for employees' actions. However, the manager must be able to delegate decision-making authority to subordinate employees in order to fulfill his or her job function. Ability D can be improved through training, but it cannot be automatically delegated.

58. D: According to Fayol's Administrative Theory of Management, the five essential functions of management are controlling, commanding, coordinating, planning, and organizing. Henri Fayol, a French engineer, pioneered the Classical Theory of Management. He argued that any individual who performed these five functions could be considered a manager, regardless of his or her actual job title.

59. D: According to the National Environmental Policy Act of 1967, a business is required to prepare an environmental impact statement (EIS) when it builds a new factory, but not when it hires a new worker, makes a charitable contribution, or develops a new marketing initiative. Environmental impact statements assess the possible environmental concerns and damage that could result from a proposed action. Hiring new workers, making charitable contributions, and even developing marketing initiatives may be important decisions from a business perspective, but they are unlikely to have any major negative impact on the environment, and thus are exempted from the EIS requirement.

60. C: A manufacturing company that implements anti-pollution measures as outlined by applicable legislation, but that opts not to introduce any additional anti-pollution measures, has most likely adopted the Social Obligation Approach to business-society relations. This means that the business will follow all applicable laws, but will not make any supplemental attempts to improve the environment or contribute to social welfare. This model is based upon cost-benefit calculations, but such calculations are not an approach to business-society relations in and of themselves. The Social Responsibility and Social Responsiveness approaches denote moderate and high levels of social involvement, respectively.

61. D: A binding contract is an agreement signed and dated by both parties, and a witness.

62. B: This situation may constitute a violation of antitrust law. If the only two oil refiners in the U.S. merged, this would mean that there would be only one oil refiner in the U.S., thus creating a monopoly. Monopolies are generally illegal because they eliminate competition that ensures fair prices for consumers.

63. C: The Equal Employment Opportunity Commission (EEOC) is responsible for enforcing Civil Rights Act of 1964, the Equal Pay Act, and the Americans with Disabilities Act, but not the Environmental Protection Act. The EEOC is primarily responsible for enforcing civil rights, while the Environmental Protection Administration (EPA) is responsible for enforcing environmental protection statutes.

64. C: Anna would need word processing software, an Internet connection, and 1-5 GB of memory. Word processing software would allow Anna to compose simple fliers and advertising materials, and an Internet connection would allow Anna to communicate with clients via email and order supplies online. 1-5 GB of memory is what standard home and small business computers need, and Quickbooks is a type of accounting software that may be useful for Anna, but would not be necessary for the tasks listed in this question.

65. D: Microsoft Excel would most likely be used to analyze numerical sales data. This software program allows users to apply mathematical formulas to numerical and categorical data. While it does also produce charts and graphs that may ultimately be used in a sales presentation, such a presentation would probably be constructed using PowerPoint.

66. C: In order to prevent unauthorized individuals from accessing confidential data, a company might require a username and password to access its computer system, and also construct a firewall to protect the computer system. By requiring passwords, the company can prevent unauthorized users such as former employees from accessing its computer system, and firewalls are designed to prevent hackers from accessing the data.

67. C: Employees may object to their social security numbers and birthdays being shared with others, and disclosing either of these could result in employee complaints and possible legal action. While information like name and work contact information must be shared in order for the business to function properly, information like Social Security numbers and birthdays is not relevant to the business, and thus should not be shared without employees' consent.

68. C: If a business education teacher has allotted one class period to help students identify potential career options, the most appropriate activity given these circumstances would be to administer a test that advises students about what careers might fit their interests and talents.

While an internship might be useful, this would not fit the allotted time period. The other two options, describing a parent's job and describing a "dream job," may also be useful. However, they are not personalized, and they do not provide students with new options that he or she may not have considered before.

69. D: Real estate agents, insurance salespeople, and financial advisors all have extensive interaction with the public and require excellent people skills. Such jobs would not be suitable for those with an aversion to working with the public.

70. D: The four most important parts of a resume are the applicant's contact information, objective, educational attainment, and relevant work experience. The contact information is crucial because it allows the employer to get in touch with the applicant, and the objective is important because it explains why the applicant is sending the resume, and what position the applicant hopes to obtain. Educational attainment and work experience are important credentials for any job, while salary requirements and employment references are typically provided in the cover letter or upon request.

71. C: The most effective way to convey information about monthly stock gains and losses over a one-year period would be to use a line graph, which would clearly indicate month-to-month changes in stock price over time. Bar and pie charts are most effective for conveying categorical information about things like market share and sector weighting, and scatter plots are usually used to show results that are comprised of many individual responses, like survey results.

72. D: When manually proofreading documents, the correct way to indicate that a section of text should be removed is to draw a horizontal line through the text with a loop at the right end. Carets are used to indicate that something should be inserted into the text, and diagonal lines are used to indicate that a letter should be lower case instead of capitalized. Xs are not standard proofreading marks.

73. B: When researching a presentation about a national shipping business, the most detailed and comprehensive source of information about the top management of the company and its competitors would most likely be Hoovers.com. LexisNexis.com is also useful for business research, but it is a searchable database of academic and news articles, rather than a database of information about specific companies and industries, like Hoovers. The local newspaper or library would be unlikely to have detailed information about competitors across the country, although it may have specific information about those located in the immediate vicinity.

74. C: Quicken, PeopleSoft, and Microsoft Office are all types of computer software. Quicken is used by individuals and small businesses for basic accounting functions, PeopleSoft is used primarily by human resources professionals, and Microsoft Office is the most widely-used word processing software on the market. The Internet is not a type of software, because it is not a program that can be installed and run on a single computer's operating system. The monitor, mouse, motherboard, and keyboard are all hardware, or equipment which is required to make software usable.

75. B: Search engine optimization (SEO) is the process of designing a website to maximize its placement in search engine results for particular keywords, thus increasing traffic to the site. Modifications are made to the website in order to make it highly relevant to certain search keywords, so that it will be among the first results Internet users see when they search for the designated keyword. This marketing tactic increases traffic to the website, and should increase sales on that website as well.

76. D: Links are used in all of the ways described here, except that they do not allow computer users to open software programs on their PC. In order to do that, one would click on an icon on one's own PC. Links, on the other hand, are inserted into a website's source code in such a way that clicking on them leads the Internet user to another website or webpage within the same site.

77. B: When designing a website for an online business, the web developer would include a site map in order to provide website users with a list of links to all of the pages on the website. Site maps, also called indexes, list each webpage that is part of the website.

78. D: Better Business Bureau certification is useful for businesses that engage in e-commerce because it reassures customers that the company is reliable and not trying to scam them. Better Business Bureau certification does not carry tax or legal protection, and the Better Business Bureau is not a governmental agency. Instead, it is a group of dues-paying members that are committed to setting and enforcing honest business practices.

79. D: Businesses can increase the security of confidential customer information by destroying paper records of credit card information, conducting employee background checks, and installing firewall and virus protection software to protect their computer systems. Firewalls and virus protection software prevent the theft of information stored on computers, and shredding paper records prevents theft as well. By conducting background checks prior to hiring employees, businesses can prevent theft by screening for individuals who have committed information or identity theft in the past.

80. D: A high school student who expresses interest in starting her own auto repair business after graduating from high school could best prepare for such a career by getting an internship or part time job at an auto-repair shop and by taking small business finance, law, and accounting courses. While experience and a basic understanding of how to run a small business would be crucial for success, a college degree and MBA would not be appropriate because they would not provide the student with the necessary industry experience she would need to be successful.

81. A: The best way for a business education teacher to evaluate her program in terms of how well graduates are prepared for the workforce would be to consult with local business leaders to find out where graduates have room for improvement. Asking students to complete internships would help prepare students for the workforce, but it would not provide the necessary feedback on students' preparedness. Surveying recent graduates would be useful, but it would provide less direct and detailed information about their performance in the workforce. Last, community college professors would be more familiar with students' performance in college courses than their performance in the workplace.

82. A: Of the activities listed here, the most effective tool for teaching business skills would be raising funds by selling concessions at athletic events. This would teach students how to attain permits and licenses, purchase and price inventory, develop a supply process, schedule employees, provide customer service, and account for sales, among many other functions that are necessary for running a small business. The other activities listed here would teach important skills, but fundraisers teach skills most directly relevant to business.

83. B: A business education teacher who is asked to serve as an advisor the local chapter of a student leadership organization is most likely to be responsible for ensuring the health and safety of student participants in the organization. In order to teach leadership and business skills,

students are usually primarily responsible for holding meetings, planning activities, and accounting for funds. Advisors are present to guide students and protect students' health and safety.

84. C: A business education teacher and a math teacher coordinating their lesson plans so that the concepts taught in math class are subsequently applied to real situations in the business class is the best example of interdisciplinary collaboration. While the other examples do require students to use skills learned in other classes like math and language arts, only example B involves active coordination between teachers in two different subject areas.

85. D: The activity that would most effectively and comprehensively assess how well students have mastered learning objectives for a unit about small business would be writing and presenting a business plan. While marketing is an important aspect of running a small business, developing a business plan would more comprehensively and directly measure and reinforce students' knowledge about small businesses.

86. D: All of the activities described here would teach skills that are necessary for working in a culturally diverse workplace. Students need to know the legal rights and responsibilities of employees and employers vis-à-vis this issue. They should also understand the perspectives of people from culturally diverse backgrounds, as well the unique problems they face in the workplace.

87. C: Based upon the information in Table 5, the correct order for the list is Business D, Business C, Business A, Business B. The triple A rating indicates the least risk, followed by double A, triple B, and double B.

88. C: If Scott Smith is paid $10 per hour on weekdays and $11 per hour on weekends, he worked a total of 16 weekday hours for $160 and 4 weekend hours for $44, for a total of $204.00.

89. C: Smith, who is a part time employee, should have social security, Medicare, and income taxes deducted from his check, because he is a W-4 employee. Since he worked less than 40 hours from November 1st through November 7th, though, he is not a full time employee and does not have health insurance or 401k deductions.

90. B: If Scott contributes 4% of his $2,000 paycheck to his 401k, this would total $80 per pay period, and the company would have to match 100% of this contribution, which would be $80.

91. C: Accounts receivable are current assets, also known as short-term assets. This term refers to open accounts that are not yet due. For example, if a landscaping company mows Anna's lawn today and the company sends her a bill for the service that is due one month later, then Anna's account would be in "account receivable" status until the due date.

92. D: Owners' equity is comprised of the amount of their initial investment in the business plus any unclaimed profits from the business' operation. (Unclaimed profits are also called retained earnings).

93. C: According to the Copyright Act of 1976, creative works like plays, poems, and architectural plans are protected by copyright law so long as they are written down. Advertising slogans are not protected because they fall under the jurisdiction of trademark law.

94. A: A phrase that is associated with a particular product would be protected by trademark law. Copyright law protects creative work, while trademarks protect business-related slogans, symbols, etc., which distinguish one product from another.

95. A: A corporation is always owned by shareholders. This means that the corporation is a separate legal entity from its shareholders. As a consequence of this, shareholders' only personal financial risk is their investment. They, unlike the corporation itself, cannot be sued by debtors if the company fails.

96. B: If an employee becomes injured because an employer did not provide equipment in good working order, this would be an example of an OSHA violation by the employer. Employees are allowed to work in hazardous conditions, so long as the employer provides adequate safety protection. Employers have the right to accompany an OSHA compliance officer on an inspection, but they are not required to do so. Employees are not covered by the OSHA act during normal commutes to and from work.

97. D: "The employee will have excellent writing skills" states the desired qualification clearly and correctly. "The employee, will have excellent oral communication skills" is incorrect because the comma is unnecessary. In the second sentence, "employee's" is possessive, and should have an apostrophe (employees'). In the third sentence, the word "well" is an adverb that would be best placed next to the verb which it modifies ("communicate well" would be correct).

98. C: The Internet is an example of a Wide Area Network (WAN). WANs are networks that cover an extremely large area. LANs (local area networks) cover smaller areas, like offices. LANs usually have faster data transfer speeds than WANs.

99. D: Nothing can be concluded from these results because students' baseline performance on these tests was not measured before the experiment. It is possible that one group of students already knew more about business, or were more academically advanced to start with. In order to account for this possibility, each group of students should have been tested prior to the beginning of the class. The effectiveness of the two teaching methods could then be compared based on the change in students' scores between the first and second test administrations.

100. C: It is illegal to employ someone under 18 in a job deemed hazardous. Such jobs include mining and manufacturing. Youths aged 16 and 17 can work in any job that is not hazardous, and youths under 14 can work in certain designated jobs like newspaper delivery and babysitting. In cases were state and federal laws conflict, the law that is more protective of minors takes precedence.

# Secret Key #1 - Time is Your Greatest Enemy

## Pace Yourself

Wear a watch. At the beginning of the test, check the time (or start a chronometer on your watch to count the minutes), and check the time after every few questions to make sure you are "on schedule."

If you are forced to speed up, do it efficiently. Usually one or more answer choices can be eliminated without too much difficulty. Above all, don't panic. Don't speed up and just begin guessing at random choices. By pacing yourself, and continually monitoring your progress against your watch, you will always know exactly how far ahead or behind you are with your available time. If you find that you are one minute behind on the test, don't skip one question without spending any time on it, just to catch back up. Take 15 fewer seconds on the next four questions, and after four questions you'll have caught back up. Once you catch back up, you can continue working each problem at your normal pace.

Furthermore, don't dwell on the problems that you were rushed on. If a problem was taking up too much time and you made a hurried guess, it must be difficult. The difficult questions are the ones you are most likely to miss anyway, so it isn't a big loss. It is better to end with more time than you need than to run out of time.

Lastly, sometimes it is beneficial to slow down if you are constantly getting ahead of time. You are always more likely to catch a careless mistake by working more slowly than quickly, and among very high-scoring test takers (those who are likely to have lots of time left over), careless errors affect the score more than mastery of material.

# Secret Key #2 - Guessing is not Guesswork

You probably know that guessing is a good idea. Unlike other standardized tests, there is no penalty for getting a wrong answer. Even if you have no idea about a question, you still have a 20-25% chance of getting it right.

Most test takers do not understand the impact that proper guessing can have on their score. Unless you score extremely high, guessing will significantly contribute to your final score.

## Monkeys Take the Test

What most test takers don't realize is that to insure that 20-25% chance, you have to guess randomly. If you put 20 monkeys in a room to take this test, assuming they answered once per question and behaved themselves, on average they would get 20-25% of the questions correct. Put 20 test takers in the room, and the average will be much lower among guessed questions. Why?
1. The test writers intentionally write deceptive answer choices that "look" right. A test taker has no idea about a question, so he picks the "best looking" answer, which is often wrong. The monkey has no idea what looks good and what doesn't, so it will consistently be right about 20-25% of the time.
2. Test takers will eliminate answer choices from the guessing pool based on a hunch or intuition. Simple but correct answers often get excluded, leaving a 0% chance of being correct. The monkey has no clue, and often gets lucky with the best choice.

This is why the process of elimination endorsed by most test courses is flawed and detrimental to your performance. Test takers don't guess; they make an ignorant stab in the dark that is usually worse than random.

# $5 Challenge

Let me introduce one of the most valuable ideas of this course—the $5 challenge:

*You only mark your "best guess" if you are willing to bet $5 on it.*
*You only eliminate choices from guessing if you are willing to bet $5 on it.*

Why $5? Five dollars is an amount of money that is small yet not insignificant, and can really add up fast (20 questions could cost you $100). Likewise, each answer choice on one question of the test will have a small impact on your overall score, but it can really add up to a lot of points in the end.

The process of elimination IS valuable. The following shows your chance of guessing it right:

| If you eliminate wrong answer choices until only this many remain: | Chance of getting it correct: |
|---|---|
| 1 | 100% |
| 2 | 50% |
| 3 | 33% |

However, if you accidentally eliminate the right answer or go on a hunch for an incorrect answer, your chances drop dramatically—to 0%. By guessing among all the answer choices, you are GUARANTEED to have a shot at the right answer.

That's why the $5 test is so valuable. If you give up the advantage and safety of a pure guess, it had better be worth the risk.

What we still haven't covered is how to be sure that whatever guess you make is truly random. Here's the easiest way:

*Always pick the first answer choice among those remaining.*

Such a technique means that you have decided, **before you see a single test question**, exactly how you are going to guess, and since the order of choices tells you nothing about which one is correct, this guessing technique is perfectly random.

This section is not meant to scare you away from making educated guesses or eliminating choices; you just need to define when a choice is worth eliminating. The $5 test, along with a pre-defined random guessing strategy, is the best way to make sure you reap all of the benefits of guessing.

# Secret Key #3 - Practice Smarter, Not Harder

Many test takers delay the test preparation process because they dread the awful amounts of practice time they think necessary to succeed on the test. We have refined an effective method that will take you only a fraction of the time.

There are a number of "obstacles" in the path to success. Among these are answering questions, finishing in time, and mastering test-taking strategies. All must be executed on the day of the test at peak performance, or your score will suffer. The test is a mental marathon that has a large impact on your future.

Just like a marathon runner, it is important to work your way up to the full challenge. So first you just worry about questions, and then time, and finally strategy:

## Success Strategy

1. Find a good source for practice tests.
2. If you are willing to make a larger time investment, consider using more than one study guide. Often the different approaches of multiple authors will help you "get" difficult concepts.
3. Take a practice test with no time constraints, with all study helps, "open book." Take your time with questions and focus on applying strategies.
4. Take a practice test with time constraints, with all guides, "open book."
5. Take a final practice test without open material and with time limits.

If you have time to take more practice tests, just repeat step 5. By gradually exposing yourself to the full rigors of the test environment, you will condition your mind to the stress of test day and maximize your success.

# Secret Key #4 - Prepare, Don't Procrastinate

Let me state an obvious fact: if you take the test three times, you will probably get three different scores. This is due to the way you feel on test day, the level of preparedness you have, and the version of the test you see. Despite the test writers' claims to the contrary, some versions of the test WILL be easier for you than others.

Since your future depends so much on your score, you should maximize your chances of success. In order to maximize the likelihood of success, you've got to prepare in advance. This means taking practice tests and spending time learning the information and test taking strategies you will need to succeed.

Never go take the actual test as a "practice" test, expecting that you can just take it again if you need to. Take all the practice tests you can on your own, but when you go to take the official test, be prepared, be focused, and do your best the first time!

# Secret Key #5 - Test Yourself

Everyone knows that time is money. There is no need to spend too much of your time or too little of your time preparing for the test. You should only spend as much of your precious time preparing as is necessary for you to get the score you need.

Once you have taken a practice test under real conditions of time constraints, then you will know if you are ready for the test or not.

If you have scored extremely high the first time that you take the practice test, then there is not much point in spending countless hours studying. You are already there.

Benchmark your abilities by retaking practice tests and seeing how much you have improved. Once you consistently score high enough to guarantee success, then you are ready.

If you have scored well below where you need, then knuckle down and begin studying in earnest. Check your improvement regularly through the use of practice tests under real conditions. Above all, don't worry, panic, or give up. The key is perseverance!

Then, when you go to take the test, remain confident and remember how well you did on the practice tests. If you can score high enough on a practice test, then you can do the same on the real thing.

# General Strategies

The most important thing you can do is to ignore your fears and jump into the test immediately. Do not be overwhelmed by any strange-sounding terms. You have to jump into the test like jumping into a pool—all at once is the easiest way.

## Make Predictions

As you read and understand the question, try to guess what the answer will be. Remember that several of the answer choices are wrong, and once you begin reading them, your mind will immediately become cluttered with answer choices designed to throw you off. Your mind is typically the most focused immediately after you have read the question and digested its contents. If you can, try to predict what the correct answer will be. You may be surprised at what you can predict.

Quickly scan the choices and see if your prediction is in the listed answer choices. If it is, then you can be quite confident that you have the right answer. It still won't hurt to check the other answer choices, but most of the time, you've got it!

## Answer the Question

It may seem obvious to only pick answer choices that answer the question, but the test writers can create some excellent answer choices that are wrong. Don't pick an answer just because it sounds right, or you believe it to be true. It MUST answer the question. Once you've made your selection, always go back and check it against the question and make sure that you didn't misread the question and that the answer choice does answer the question posed.

## Benchmark

After you read the first answer choice, decide if you think it sounds correct or not. If it doesn't, move on to the next answer choice. If it does, mentally mark that answer choice. This doesn't mean that you've definitely selected it as your answer choice, it just means that it's the best you've seen thus far. Go ahead and read the next choice. If the next choice is worse than the one you've already selected, keep going to the next answer choice. If the next choice is better than the choice you've already selected, mentally mark the new answer choice as your best guess.

The first answer choice that you select becomes your standard. Every other answer choice must be benchmarked against that standard. That choice is correct until proven otherwise by another answer choice beating it out. Once you've decided that no other answer choice seems as good, do one final check to ensure that your answer choice answers the question posed.

## Valid Information

Don't discount any of the information provided in the question. Every piece of information may be necessary to determine the correct answer. None of the information in the question is there to throw you off (while the answer choices will certainly have information to throw you off). If two seemingly unrelated topics are discussed, don't ignore either. You can be confident there is a relationship, or it wouldn't be included in the question, and you are probably going to have to determine what is that relationship to find the answer.

## Avoid "Fact Traps"

Don't get distracted by a choice that is factually true. Your search is for the answer that answers the question. Stay focused and don't fall for an answer that is true but irrelevant. Always go back to the question and make sure you're choosing an answer that actually answers the question and is not just a true statement. An answer can be factually correct, but it MUST answer the question asked. Additionally, two answers can both be seemingly correct, so be sure to read all of the answer choices, and make sure that you get the one that BEST answers the question.

## Milk the Question

Some of the questions may throw you completely off. They might deal with a subject you have not been exposed to, or one that you haven't reviewed in years. While your lack of knowledge about the subject will be a hindrance, the question itself can give you many clues that will help you find the correct answer. Read the question carefully and look for clues. Watch particularly for adjectives and nouns describing difficult terms or words that you don't recognize. Regardless of whether you completely understand a word or not, replacing it with a synonym, either provided or one you more familiar with, may help you to understand what the questions are asking. Rather than wracking your mind about specific detailed information concerning a difficult term or word, try to use mental substitutes that are easier to understand.

## The Trap of Familiarity

Don't just choose a word because you recognize it. On difficult questions, you may not recognize a number of words in the answer choices. The test writers don't put "make-believe" words on the test, so don't think that just because you only recognize all the words in one answer choice that that answer choice must be correct. If you only recognize words in one answer choice, then focus on that one. Is it correct? Try your best to determine if it is correct. If it is, that's great. If not, eliminate it. Each word and answer choice you eliminate increases your chances of getting the question correct, even if you then have to guess among the unfamiliar choices.

## Eliminate Answers

Eliminate choices as soon as you realize they are wrong. But be careful! Make sure you consider all of the possible answer choices. Just because one appears right, doesn't mean that the next one won't be even better! The test writers will usually put more than one good answer choice for every question, so read all of them. Don't worry if you are stuck between two that seem right. By getting down to just two remaining possible choices, your odds are now 50/50. Rather than wasting too much time, play the odds. You are guessing, but guessing wisely because you've been able to knock out some of the answer choices that you know are wrong. If you are eliminating choices and realize that the last answer choice you are left with is also obviously wrong, don't panic. Start over and consider each choice again. There may easily be something that you missed the first time and will realize on the second pass.

## Tough Questions

If you are stumped on a problem or it appears too hard or too difficult, don't waste time. Move on! Remember though, if you can quickly check for obviously incorrect answer choices, your chances of guessing correctly are greatly improved. Before you completely give up, at least try to knock out a couple of possible answers. Eliminate what you can and then guess at the remaining answer choices before moving on.

## Brainstorm

If you get stuck on a difficult question, spend a few seconds quickly brainstorming. Run through the complete list of possible answer choices. Look at each choice and ask yourself, "Could this answer the question satisfactorily?" Go through each answer choice and consider it independently of the others. By systematically going through all possibilities, you may find something that you would otherwise overlook. Remember though that when you get stuck, it's important to try to keep moving.

## Read Carefully

Understand the problem. Read the question and answer choices carefully. Don't miss the question because you misread the terms. You have plenty of time to read each question thoroughly and make sure you understand what is being asked. Yet a happy medium must be attained, so don't waste too much time. You must read carefully, but efficiently.

## Face Value

When in doubt, use common sense. Always accept the situation in the problem at face value. Don't read too much into it. These problems will not require you to make huge leaps of logic. The test writers aren't trying to throw you off with a cheap trick. If you have to go beyond creativity and make a leap of logic in order to have an answer choice answer the question, then you should look at the other answer choices. Don't overcomplicate the problem by creating theoretical relationships or explanations that will warp time or space. These are normal problems rooted in reality. It's just that the applicable relationship or explanation may not be readily apparent and you have to figure things out. Use your common sense to interpret anything that isn't clear.

## Prefixes

If you're having trouble with a word in the question or answer choices, try dissecting it. Take advantage of every clue that the word might include. Prefixes and suffixes can be a huge help. Usually they allow you to determine a basic meaning. Pre- means before, post- means after, pro - is positive, de- is negative. From these prefixes and suffixes, you can get an idea of the general meaning of the word and try to put it into context. Beware though of any traps. Just because con- is the opposite of pro-, doesn't necessarily mean congress is the opposite of progress!

## Hedge Phrases

Watch out for critical hedge phrases, led off with words such as "likely," "may," "can," "sometimes," "often," "almost," "mostly," "usually," "generally," "rarely," and "sometimes." Question writers insert these hedge phrases to cover every possibility. Often an answer choice will be wrong simply because it leaves no room for exception. Unless the situation calls for them, avoid answer choices that have definitive words like "exactly," and "always."

## Switchback Words

Stay alert for "switchbacks." These are the words and phrases frequently used to alert you to shifts in thought. The most common switchback word is "but." Others include "although," "however," "nevertheless," "on the other hand," "even though," "while," "in spite of," "despite," and "regardless of."

## New Information

Correct answer choices will rarely have completely new information included. Answer choices typically are straightforward reflections of the material asked about and will directly relate to the question. If a new piece of information is included in an answer choice that doesn't even seem to relate to the topic being asked about, then that answer choice is likely incorrect. All of the information needed to answer the question is usually provided for you in the question. You should not have to make guesses that are unsupported or choose answer choices that require unknown information that cannot be reasoned from what is given.

## Time Management

On technical questions, don't get lost on the technical terms. Don't spend too much time on any one question. If you don't know what a term means, then odds are you aren't going to get much further since you don't have a dictionary. You should be able to immediately recognize whether or not you know a term. If you don't, work with the other clues that you have—the other answer choices and terms provided—but don't waste too much time trying to figure out a difficult term that you don't know.

## Contextual Clues

Look for contextual clues. An answer can be right but not the correct answer. The contextual clues will help you find the answer that is most right and is correct. Understand the context in which a phrase or statement is made. This will help you make important distinctions.

## Don't Panic

Panicking will not answer any questions for you; therefore, it isn't helpful. When you first see the question, if your mind goes blank, take a deep breath. Force yourself to mechanically go through the steps of solving the problem using the strategies you've learned.

## Pace Yourself

Don't get clock fever. It's easy to be overwhelmed when you're looking at a page full of questions, your mind is full of random thoughts and feeling confused, and the clock is ticking down faster than you would like. Calm down and maintain the pace that you have set for yourself. As long as you are on track by monitoring your pace, you are guaranteed to have enough time for yourself. When you get to the last few minutes of the test, it may seem like you won't have enough time left, but if you only have as many questions as you should have left at that point, then you're right on track!

## Answer Selection

The best way to pick an answer choice is to eliminate all of those that are wrong, until only one is left and confirm that is the correct answer. Sometimes though, an answer choice may immediately look right. Be careful! Take a second to make sure that the other choices are not equally obvious. Don't make a hasty mistake. There are only two times that you should stop before checking other answers. First is when you are positive that the answer choice you have selected is correct. Second is when time is almost out and you have to make a quick guess!

## Check Your Work

Since you will probably not know every term listed and the answer to every question, it is important that you get credit for the ones that you do know. Don't miss any questions through careless mistakes. If at all possible, try to take a second to look back over your answer selection and make sure you've selected the correct answer choice and haven't made a costly careless mistake (such as marking an answer choice that you didn't mean to mark). The time it takes for this quick double check should more than pay for itself in caught mistakes.

## Beware of Directly Quoted Answers

Sometimes an answer choice will repeat word for word a portion of the question or reference section. However, beware of such exact duplication. It may be a trap! More than likely, the correct choice will paraphrase or summarize a point, rather than being exactly the same wording.

## Slang

Scientific sounding answers are better than slang ones. An answer choice that begins "To compare the outcomes…" is much more likely to be correct than one that begins "Because some people insisted…"

## Extreme Statements

Avoid wild answers that throw out highly controversial ideas that are proclaimed as established fact. An answer choice that states the "process should used in certain situations, if…" is much more likely to be correct than one that states the "process should be discontinued completely." The first is a calm rational statement and doesn't even make a definitive, uncompromising stance, using a hedge word "if" to provide wiggle room, whereas the second choice is a radical idea and far more extreme.

## Answer Choice Families

When you have two or more answer choices that are direct opposites or parallels, one of them is usually the correct answer. For instance, if one answer choice states "x increases" and another answer choice states "x decreases" or "y increases," then those two or three answer choices are very similar in construction and fall into the same family of answer choices. A family of answer choices consists of two or three answer choices, very similar in construction, but often with directly opposite meanings. Usually the correct answer choice will be in that family of answer choices. The "odd man out" or answer choice that doesn't seem to fit the parallel construction of the other answer choices is more likely to be incorrect.

# Special Report: How to Overcome Test Anxiety

The very nature of tests caters to some level of anxiety, nervousness, or tension, just as we feel for any important event that occurs in our lives. A little bit of anxiety or nervousness can be a good thing. It helps us with motivation, and makes achievement just that much sweeter. However, too much anxiety can be a problem, especially if it hinders our ability to function and perform.

"Test anxiety," is the term that refers to the emotional reactions that some test-takers experience when faced with a test or exam. Having a fear of testing and exams is based upon a rational fear, since the test-taker's performance can shape the course of an academic career. Nevertheless, experiencing excessive fear of examinations will only interfere with the test-taker's ability to perform and chance to be successful.

There are a large variety of causes that can contribute to the development and sensation of test anxiety. These include, but are not limited to, lack of preparation and worrying about issues surrounding the test.

## Lack of Preparation

Lack of preparation can be identified by the following behaviors or situations:

Not scheduling enough time to study, and therefore cramming the night before the test or exam
Managing time poorly, to create the sensation that there is not enough time to do everything
Failing to organize the text information in advance, so that the study material consists of the entire text and not simply the pertinent information
Poor overall studying habits

Worrying, on the other hand, can be related to both the test taker, or many other factors around him/her that will be affected by the results of the test. These include worrying about:

Previous performances on similar exams, or exams in general
How friends and other students are achieving
The negative consequences that will result from a poor grade or failure

There are three primary elements to test anxiety. Physical components, which involve the same typical bodily reactions as those to acute anxiety (to be discussed below). Emotional factors have to do with fear or panic. Mental or cognitive issues concerning attention spans and memory abilities.

# Physical Signals

There are many different symptoms of test anxiety, and these are not limited to mental and emotional strain.  Frequently there are a range of physical signals that will let a test taker know that he/she is suffering from test anxiety.  These bodily changes can include the following:

Perspiring
Sweaty palms
Wet, trembling hands
Nausea
Dry mouth
A knot in the stomach
Headache
Faintness
Muscle tension
Aching shoulders, back and neck
Rapid heart beat
Feeling too hot/cold

To recognize the sensation of test anxiety, a test-taker should monitor him/herself for the following sensations:

The physical distress symptoms as listed above
Emotional sensitivity, expressing emotional feelings such as the need to cry or laugh too much, or a sensation of anger or helplessness
A decreased ability to think, causing the test-taker to blank out or have racing thoughts that are hard to organize or control.

Though most students will feel some level of anxiety when faced with a test or exam, the majority can cope with that anxiety and maintain it at a manageable level.  However, those who cannot are faced with a very real and very serious condition, which can and should be controlled for the immeasurable benefit of this sufferer.

Naturally, these sensations lead to negative results for the testing experience.  The most common effects of test anxiety have to do with nervousness and mental blocking.

# Nervousness

Nervousness can appear in several different levels:

The test-taker's difficulty, or even inability to read and understand the questions on the test
The difficulty or inability to organize thoughts to a coherent form
The difficulty or inability to recall key words and concepts relating to the testing questions (especially essays)
The receipt of poor grades on a test, though the test material was well known by the test taker

Conversely, a person may also experience mental blocking, which involves:

Blanking out on test questions
Only remembering the correct answers to the questions when the test has already finished.

Fortunately for test anxiety sufferers, beating these feelings, to a large degree, has to do with proper preparation. When a test taker has a feeling of preparedness, then anxiety will be dramatically lessened.

The first step to resolving anxiety issues is to distinguish which of the two types of anxiety are being suffered. If the anxiety is a direct result of a lack of preparation, this should be considered a normal reaction, and the anxiety level (as opposed to the test results) shouldn't be anything to worry about. However, if, when adequately prepared, the test-taker still panics, blanks out, or seems to overreact, this is not a fully rational reaction. While this can be considered normal too, there are many ways to combat and overcome these effects.

Remember that anxiety cannot be entirely eliminated, however, there are ways to minimize it, to make the anxiety easier to manage. Preparation is one of the best ways to minimize test anxiety. Therefore the following techniques are wise in order to best fight off any anxiety that may want to build.

To begin with, try to avoid cramming before a test, whenever it is possible. By trying to memorize an entire term's worth of information in one day, you'll be shocking your system, and not giving yourself a very good chance to absorb the information. This is an easy path to anxiety, so for those who suffer from test anxiety, cramming should not even be considered an option.

Instead of cramming, work throughout the semester to combine all of the material which is presented throughout the semester, and work on it gradually as the course goes by, making sure to master the main concepts first, leaving minor details for a week or so before the test.

To study for the upcoming exam, be sure to pose questions that may be on the examination, to gauge the ability to answer them by integrating the ideas from your texts, notes and lectures, as well as any supplementary readings.

If it is truly impossible to cover all of the information that was covered in that particular term, concentrate on the most important portions, that can be covered very well. Learn these concepts as best as possible, so that when the test comes, a goal can be made to use these concepts as presentations of your knowledge.

In addition to study habits, changes in attitude are critical to beating a struggle with test anxiety. In fact, an improvement of the perspective over the entire test-taking experience can actually help a test taker to enjoy studying and therefore improve the overall experience. Be certain not to overemphasize the significance of the grade - know that the result of the test is neither a reflection of self worth, nor is it a measure of intelligence; one grade will not predict a person's future success.

To improve an overall testing outlook, the following steps should be tried:

Keeping in mind that the most reasonable expectation for taking a test is to expect to try to demonstrate as much of what you know as you possibly can.

Reminding ourselves that a test is only one test; this is not the only one, and there will be others.

The thought of thinking of oneself in an irrational, all-or-nothing term should be avoided at all costs.

A reward should be designated for after the test, so there's something to look forward to. Whether it be going to a movie, going out to eat, or simply visiting friends, schedule it in advance, and do it no matter what result is expected on the exam.

Test-takers should also keep in mind that the basics are some of the most important things, even beyond anti-anxiety techniques and studying. Never neglect the basic social, emotional and biological needs, in order to try to absorb information. In order to best achieve, these three factors must be held as just as important as the studying itself.

## Study Steps

Remember the following important steps for studying:

Maintain healthy nutrition and exercise habits. Continue both your recreational activities and social pass times. These both contribute to your physical and emotional well being.
Be certain to get a good amount of sleep, especially the night before the test, because when you're overtired you are not able to perform to the best of your best ability.
Keep the studying pace to a moderate level by taking breaks when they are needed, and varying the work whenever possible, to keep the mind fresh instead of getting bored.
When enough studying has been done that all the material that can be learned has been learned, and the test taker is prepared for the test, stop studying and do something relaxing such as listening to music, watching a movie, or taking a warm bubble bath.

There are also many other techniques to minimize the uneasiness or apprehension that is experienced along with test anxiety before, during, or even after the examination. In fact, there are a great deal of things that can be done to stop anxiety from interfering with lifestyle and performance. Again, remember that anxiety will not be eliminated entirely, and it shouldn't be. Otherwise that "up" feeling for exams would not exist, and most of us depend on that sensation to perform better than usual. However, this anxiety has to be at a level that is manageable.

Of course, as we have just discussed, being prepared for the exam is half the battle right away. Attending all classes, finding out what knowledge will be expected on the exam, and knowing the exam schedules are easy steps to lowering anxiety. Keeping up with work will remove the need to cram, and efficient study habits will eliminate wasted time. Studying should be done in an ideal location for concentration, so that it is simple to become interested in the material and give it complete attention. A method such as SQ3R (Survey, Question, Read, Recite, Review) is a wonderful key to follow to make sure that the study habits are as effective as possible, especially in the case of learning from a textbook. Flashcards are great techniques for memorization. Learning to take good notes will mean that notes will be full of useful information, so that less sifting will need to be done to seek out what is pertinent for studying. Reviewing notes after class and then again on occasion will keep the information fresh in the mind. From notes that have been taken summary sheets and outlines can be made for simpler reviewing.

A study group can also be a very motivational and helpful place to study, as there will be a sharing of ideas, all of the minds can work together, to make sure that everyone understands, and the studying will be made more interesting because it will be a social occasion.

Basically, though, as long as the test-taker remains organized and self confident, with efficient study habits, less time will need to be spent studying, and higher grades will be achieved.

To become self confident, there are many useful steps. The first of these is "self talk." It has been shown through extensive research, that self-talk for students who suffer from test anxiety, should be well monitored, in order to make sure that it contributes to self confidence as opposed to sinking the student. Frequently the self talk of test-anxious students is negative or self-defeating, thinking that everyone else is smarter and faster, that they always mess up, and that if they don't do well, they'll fail the entire course. It is important to decreasing anxiety that awareness is made of self talk. Try writing any negative self thoughts and then disputing them with a positive statement instead. Begin self-encouragement as though it was a friend speaking. Repeat positive statements to help reprogram the mind to believing in successes instead of failures.

## Helpful Techniques

Other extremely helpful techniques include:

Self-visualization of doing well and reaching goals
While aiming for an "A" level of understanding, don't try to "overprotect" by setting your expectations lower. This will only convince the mind to stop studying in order to meet the lower expectations.
Don't make comparisons with the results or habits of other students. These are individual factors, and different things work for different people, causing different results.
Strive to become an expert in learning what works well, and what can be done in order to improve. Consider collecting this data in a journal.
Create rewards for after studying instead of doing things before studying that will only turn into avoidance behaviors.
Make a practice of relaxing - by using methods such as progressive relaxation, self-hypnosis, guided imagery, etc - in order to make relaxation an automatic sensation.
Work on creating a state of relaxed concentration so that concentrating will take on the focus of the mind, so that none will be wasted on worrying.
Take good care of the physical self by eating well and getting enough sleep.
Plan in time for exercise and stick to this plan.

Beyond these techniques, there are other methods to be used before, during and after the test that will help the test-taker perform well in addition to overcoming anxiety.

Before the exam comes the academic preparation. This involves establishing a study schedule and beginning at least one week before the actual date of the test. By doing this, the anxiety of not having enough time to study for the test will be automatically eliminated. Moreover, this will make the studying a much more effective experience, ensuring that the learning will be an easier process. This relieves much undue pressure on the test-taker.

Summary sheets, note cards, and flash cards with the main concepts and examples of these main concepts should be prepared in advance of the actual studying time. A topic should never be eliminated from this process. By omitting a topic because it isn't expected to be on the test is only setting up the test-taker for anxiety should it actually appear on the exam. Utilize the course syllabus for laying out the topics that should be studied. Carefully go over the notes that were made in class, paying special attention to any of the issues that the professor took special care to emphasize while lecturing in class. In the textbooks, use the chapter review, or if possible, the chapter tests, to begin your review.

It may even be possible to ask the instructor what information will be covered on the exam, or what the format of the exam will be (for example, multiple choice, essay, free form, true-false). Additionally, see if it is possible to find out how many questions will be on the test. If a review sheet or sample test has been offered by the professor, make good use of it, above anything else, for the preparation for the test. Another great resource for getting to know the examination is reviewing tests from previous semesters. Use these tests to review, and aim to achieve a 100% score on each of the possible topics. With a few exceptions, the goal that you set for yourself is the highest one that you will reach.

Take all of the questions that were assigned as homework, and rework them to any other possible course material. The more problems reworked, the more skill and confidence will form as a result. When forming the solution to a problem, write out each of the steps. Don't simply do head work. By doing as many steps on paper as possible, much clarification and therefore confidence will be formed. Do this with as many homework problems as possible, before checking the answers. By checking the answer after each problem, a reinforcement will exist, that will not be on the exam. Study situations should be as exam-like as possible, to prime the test-taker's system for the experience. By waiting to check the answers at the end, a psychological advantage will be formed, to decrease the stress factor.

Another fantastic reason for not cramming is the avoidance of confusion in concepts, especially when it comes to mathematics. 8-10 hours of study will become one hundred percent more effective if it is spread out over a week or at least several days, instead of doing it all in one sitting. Recognize that the human brain requires time in order to assimilate new material, so frequent breaks and a span of study time over several days will be much more beneficial.

Additionally, don't study right up until the point of the exam. Studying should stop a minimum of one hour before the exam begins. This allows the brain to rest and put things in their proper order. This will also provide the time to become as relaxed as possible when going into the examination room. The test-taker will also have time to eat well and eat sensibly. Know that the brain needs food as much as the rest of the body. With enough food and enough sleep, as well as a relaxed attitude, the body and the mind are primed for success.

Avoid any anxious classmates who are talking about the exam. These students only spread anxiety, and are not worth sharing the anxious sentimentalities.

Before the test also involves creating a positive attitude, so mental preparation should also be a point of concentration. There are many keys to creating a positive attitude. Should fears become rushing in, make a visualization of taking the exam, doing well, and seeing an A written on the paper. Write out a list of affirmations that will bring a feeling of confidence, such as "I am doing well in my English class," "I studied well and know my material," "I enjoy this class." Even if the affirmations aren't believed at first, it sends a positive message to the subconscious which will result in an alteration of the overall belief system, which is the system that creates reality.

If a sensation of panic begins, work with the fear and imagine the very worst! Work through the entire scenario of not passing the test, failing the entire course, and dropping out of school, followed by not getting a job, and pushing a shopping cart through the dark alley where you'll live. This will place things into perspective! Then, practice deep breathing and create a visualization of the opposite situation - achieving an "A" on the exam, passing the entire course, receiving the degree at a graduation ceremony.

On the day of the test, there are many things to be done to ensure the best results, as well as the most calm outlook. The following stages are suggested in order to maximize test-taking potential:

Begin the examination day with a moderate breakfast, and avoid any coffee or beverages with caffeine if the test taker is prone to jitters. Even people who are used to managing caffeine can feel jittery or light-headed when it is taken on a test day.
Attempt to do something that is relaxing before the examination begins. As last minute cramming clouds the mastering of overall concepts, it is better to use this time to create a calming outlook.
Be certain to arrive at the test location well in advance, in order to provide time to select a location that is away from doors, windows and other distractions, as well as giving enough time to relax before the test begins.
Keep away from anxiety generating classmates who will upset the sensation of stability and relaxation that is being attempted before the exam.
Should the waiting period before the exam begins cause anxiety, create a self-distraction by reading a light magazine or something else that is relaxing and simple.

During the exam itself, read the entire exam from beginning to end, and find out how much time should be allotted to each individual problem. Once writing the exam, should more time be taken for a problem, it should be abandoned, in order to begin another problem. If there is time at the end, the unfinished problem can always be returned to and completed.

Read the instructions very carefully - twice - so that unpleasant surprises won't follow during or after the exam has ended.

When writing the exam, pretend that the situation is actually simply the completion of homework within a library, or at home. This will assist in forming a relaxed atmosphere, and will allow the brain extra focus for the complex thinking function.

Begin the exam with all of the questions with which the most confidence is felt. This will build the confidence level regarding the entire exam and will begin a quality momentum. This will also create encouragement for trying the problems where uncertainty resides.

Going with the "gut instinct" is always the way to go when solving a problem. Second guessing should be avoided at all costs. Have confidence in the ability to do well.

For essay questions, create an outline in advance that will keep the mind organized and make certain that all of the points are remembered. For multiple choice, read every answer, even if the correct one has been spotted - a better one may exist.

Continue at a pace that is reasonable and not rushed, in order to be able to work carefully. Provide enough time to go over the answers at the end, to check for small errors that can be corrected.

Should a feeling of panic begin, breathe deeply, and think of the feeling of the body releasing sand through its pores. Visualize a calm, peaceful place, and include all of the sights, sounds and sensations of this image. Continue the deep breathing, and take a few minutes to continue this with closed eyes. When all is well again, return to the test.

If a "blanking" occurs for a certain question, skip it and move on to the next question. There will be time to return to the other question later. Get everything done that can be done, first, to guarantee all the grades that can be compiled, and to build all of the confidence possible. Then return to the weaker questions to build the marks from there.

Remember, one's own reality can be created, so as long as the belief is there, success will follow. And remember: anxiety can happen later, right now, there's an exam to be written!

After the examination is complete, whether there is a feeling for a good grade or a bad grade, don't dwell on the exam, and be certain to follow through on the reward that was promised...and enjoy it! Don't dwell on any mistakes that have been made, as there is nothing that can be done at this point anyway.

Additionally, don't begin to study for the next test right away. Do something relaxing for a while, and let the mind relax and prepare itself to begin absorbing information again.

From the results of the exam - both the grade and the entire experience, be certain to learn from what has gone on. Perfect studying habits and work some more on confidence in order to make the next examination experience even better than the last one.

Learn to avoid places where openings occurred for laziness, procrastination and day dreaming.

Use the time between this exam and the next one to better learn to relax, even learning to relax on cue, so that any anxiety can be controlled during the next exam. Learn how to relax the body. Slouch in your chair if that helps. Tighten and then relax all of the different muscle groups, one group at a time, beginning with the feet and then working all the way up to the neck and face. This will ultimately relax the muscles more than they were to begin with. Learn how to breathe deeply and comfortably, and focus on this breathing going in and out as a relaxing thought. With every exhale, repeat the word "relax."

As common as test anxiety is, it is very possible to overcome it. Make yourself one of the test-takers who overcome this frustrating hindrance.

# Additional Bonus Material

Due to our efforts to try to keep this book to a manageable length, we've created a link that will give you access to all of your additional bonus material.

Please visit http://www.mometrix.com/bonus948/priibusedck to access the information.

Made in the USA
Middletown, DE
03 August 2017